# AN INTRODUCTION TO DRAMATHERAPY

D0141186

# CREATIVE THERAPIES IN PRACTICE

The *Creative Therapies in Practice* series, edited by Paul Wilkins, introduces and explores a range of arts therapies, providing trainees and practitioners alike with a comprehensive overview of theory and practice. Drawing on case material to demonstrate the methods and techniques involved, the books are lively and informative introductions to using the creative arts in therapeutic practice.

Books in the series:

# AN INTRODUCTION TO DRAMATHERAPY

## *Dorothy Langley*

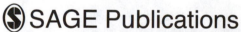

# SAGE Publications
London • Thousand Oaks • New Delhi

SAGE Publications Ltd
1 Oliver's Yard
55 City Road
London EC1Y 1SP

SAGE Publications Inc.
2455 Teller Road
Thousand Oaks, California 91320

SAGE Publications India Pvt Ltd
B-42, Panchsheel Enclave
Post Box 4109
New Delhi 110 017

**British Library Cataloguing in Publication data**

A catalogue record for this book is available
from the British Library

ISBN-10 0-7619-5976-9          ISBN-13 978-0-7619-5976-2
ISBN-10 0-7619-5977-7 (pbk)    ISBN-13 978-0-7619-5977-9 (pbk)

**Library of Congress Control Number available**

Typeset by C&M Digitals (P) Ltd., Chennai, India
Printed on paper from sustainable resources
Printed in India by Gopsons Papers Ltd, Noida

# CONTENTS

# ACKNOWLEDGEMENTS

I would like to thank a number of people for their assistance:

- Paul Wilkins, the series editor, for his help in producing this book and making valuable suggestions drawn from his broad knowledge of psychotherapy;
- Leon Winston for reading several drafts of this work;
- Georgette Zackey for keeping me to the task;
- Anne Bannister, Di Gammage, Alida Gersie, Jessica Williams Saunders and Sarah Scoble for their helpful advice;
- Members of Creative Connections, South West who have willingly shared their experiences – Paul Bateson, Mary Booker, Lynne Cook, Ian Hegginworth, Chris Hill, Sara Jarman, Hazel McMahan and Nik Pitcher.
- The many clients, students and colleagues throughout my professional career from whom I have learned so much about the dynamics and process of dramatherapy.

Above all I want to thank my husband, Gordon, for his tireless reading of so many drafts, his help with baffling technology and for his love and support throughout.

# INTRODUCTION

This book addresses five questions I am frequently asked:

1 What is dramatherapy?
2 What do dramatherapists do?
3 Who can benefit from dramatherapy?
4 Where do dramatherapists work?
5 How does one become a dramatherapist?

It portrays the practice of dramatherapists and their clients as well as the dramatherapeutic process.

Dramatherapists in the UK are professionals who are trained in both drama and therapy. They are regulated by the Health Professions Council (HPC) as Arts Therapists, jointly with Music, Art, and Dance Movement Therapists. From April 2003 'dramatherapist' became a protected title and it is now unlawful to call oneself a 'dramatherapist' unless registered with the HPC.

As with other professional organisations, the British Association of Dramatherapists has some expectations and requirements of its practitioners, namely that:

1 Their training is approved and inspected by the Health Professions Council
2 Trained dramatherapists, as well as students, regularly review their practice with another experienced professional in a supervision session
3 Dramatherapists engage in continued professional development after training to maintain levels of competence
4 They enter into personal therapy when it is required, in order not to confuse their own issues with those of their clients
5 They abide by a code of practice issued by the Association.

Personal therapy is important during training to deal with any personal issues that may cloud judgement as a therapist, and also to learn the therapy 'from the inside'. Professional development after training allows one to continue learning informally and the code of practice ensures ethical behaviour.

Throughout this book, vignettes describing examples of therapeutic situations are described. Most of them are from my own experience, or occasionally from those of my colleagues. Names have been changed, situations amalgamated and fictionalised in order to preserve confidentiality. They are none-the-less typical of practice.

# 1

# WHAT IS DRAMATHERAPY?

Dramatherapy is a method of therapy which uses the dramatic process to help people during times of stress, emotional upheaval or disability. The techniques of dramatherapy are described in detail in Chapter 2 but, broadly speaking and according to their applicability, they are the techniques of drama and theatre in all their many forms. These include role play, enaction (either using scripts or by improvisation), the use of puppets and masks, storytelling, the use of rituals and games and much, much more.

In dramatherapy, the employment of drama and theatre as a medium for change during the course of illness, crisis or uncertainty, or to facilitate personal growth is *intentional* and is the essence of the approach. This intention differentiates it from other forms of dramatic activity. The therapeutic element is in the *process* of dramatic art, not the final enactment, so emphasis is on the experience and not the standard of performance (Langley and Langley, 1983: 14).

'Intention' is the important word; change does not happen by chance. Theatre and drama can be randomly therapeutic because they raise awareness to issues, attitudes and one's own emotions. There is value in this in other fields, such as education and social learning, but dramatherapy is a deliberate application in order to alter attitudes, change behaviour and help with confronting and dealing with psychological disorders or emotional or behavioural enlightenment. It can be used to help people come to terms with permanent disability as well as ameliorate temporary illness and problems in times of crisis. Before considering who can benefit from dramatherapy it is necessary to have a clear definition of its purpose. The expectation for therapy or healing in its strictest sense is 'to cure or comfort'. Expressed in broader and more realistic terms, it is now accepted that therapy is concerned with change. It can mean healing in the sense of relief or cure, a change of perspective or behaviour, adaptation to disability, coming to terms with reality, or simply personal growth. Dramatherapy has the potential to effect change in a wide spectrum of conditions and problems if applied and conducted appropriately. Dramatherapy is directed towards an individual or group of people and usually focuses on a particular issue. In order to do this, the dramatherapist needs to form a special relationship with the client based on mutual trust. It is the awareness of the intent by client and therapist that affirms the difference between dramatherapy and drama.

The important elements of dramatherapy then are that it is an intentional and directional use of drama with the expressed purpose of effecting constructive change. One of the advantages of dramatherapy is that there is no right or wrong way of doing it, apart from the confines of confidentiality and boundaries common to all psychotherapies. If the client interprets the instruction or medium in a way that is not intended, it does not matter unless the dramatherapy session is directed towards special learning, such as social skills. Their understanding may be more important to them personally than the dramatherapist's original idea. The important issues, for the client and/or the group will become obvious and can be tackled, either at the time or in a later session. As with all psychotherapy, dramatherapy is only effective when there is a trusting relationship between the therapist and the individual client or group.

Not all clients come with an agenda of disorder or disturbance. Many people today seek a clearer understanding of themselves and their personal issues. Most of us feel the need to examine situations or feelings at some time. Drama is an excellent medium for exploration because of its metaphoric foundation. Clients can consider their lives, relationships and the issues around them by finding a metaphor, exploring it and then connecting their experience to reality. It also encourages a state of personal awareness which, although not necessarily healing in the strict sense of cure, is a means of working towards establishing peace of mind and/or improved functioning. In order to deal with their own issues, and also understand the dramatherapeutic process, all dramatherapists in training in the UK have to undergo their own personal therapy. Part of that therapy must be group dramatherapy, part must be individual therapy.

Although drama and dramatherapy are different things, it is only by understanding the origins and development of drama and theatre that dramatherapy itself comes into proper perspective.

## The origins of drama

The development of dramatherapy is closely associated with the evolution of drama itself and an understanding of the latter is essential to comprehending the former. Related to drama is *theatre* and both terms are used in this book. For the sake of clarity throughout, the distinction is made between *drama* as being physical expression and enactment in general, and *theatre* as having a specific structure of performers separated from spectators, usually with a discrete performance area or stage.

Although the origins of drama are obscure, Hunningher (1955) has written widely about the subject in *The Origins of Theatre*, maintaining that there is no doubt it was originally a communal game and a form of adult play which developed into ritual comprising dances (Hunningher, 1955: 15). Harrison had previously asserted that in time these dances became dramatic or artistic representations (Harrison, 1913: 28). Such portrayals started as a re-enactment of tribal activities during the hunt or at war. Hunningher (1955: 18) takes the view that, prior to the development of language, these rituals were a means of reporting events. As communication evolved, the dances became *rehearsals*, culminating in a belief that the good-will of the appropriate god would be ensured by the dance, so introducing the elements of religion and magic (Harrison, 1913: 44). The dances were essentially group activities. Communal effort was essential to the life and well-being of the tribe and provided a vehicle for solving problems and answering prayers. The expression and relief of emotional tension are fundamental elements of ritual and also of art. Both originate from the desire to represent emotion by metaphor (Harrison, 1913: 26). In many ways, it is this representation of emotional issues through metaphor which underpins the practice of dramatherapy and which allows 'therapeutic distance'.

It was the Greeks who coined the term *drama* – their word for action or 'a thing done' – and from drama, theatre evolved. Theatre is seen as evolving from the ritual of the 'Year Dances' at the end of winter and the coming of spring. These rituals developed into narrative dances of hunting and battle heroes. In these ritual dances, the performers no longer danced as themselves, but took on the role of another person, animal, spirit or other being. The gradual separation of ritual and theatre was initiated as myths began to evolve around these heroes (Hunningher, 1955: 28). When the participants became more sophisticated and no longer believed in ritual magic, some people ceased to participate. They became spectators at a performance. A space was made for these spectators who became more distanced, were inactive, yet still involved both cognitively and emotionally – *theatre* was born (Hunningher, 1955: 43). At this point, the proceedings became *art* not ritual – the *art of theatre* (Harrison, 1913: 126/7). Yet there still remains an element of ritual to this day, the very act of going to the theatre can be seen as ritual and the same involvement of the audience is still paramount.

The progression from ritual to theatre was probably slow and is epitomised by the evolution of Greek theatre which ultimately developed from the worship of the god Dionysus and the dithyramb, or hymn that was sung around his altar. This was a corporate event, with a chorus of 50 members who told or enacted the story (Hartnoll, 1985: 8). The number became varied over a period of time until, it is popularly believed, one actor, Thespis, stepped out from the chorus to enact an individual character, ending the long tradition and making way for solo actors to take the stage. The move was an important one in that group activity gave way to individual presentation, leading to the creation of Greek tragedy. This transition has been described as a 'leap towards theatre' rather than its gradual development as the progression itself was dramatic (Else, 1965: 3). The shift from choral storytelling to enacted plays created an accessible means of personal identification as people recognised their own issues and feelings represented on stage. This means of empathising with fictional characters 'as if' they were real allowed the audience to view their own problems from a distance, thus facilitating the development of the therapeutic aspects of drama.

The evolution of Greek theatre is often described as the main period of theatrical development and also the place where its therapeutic value was first acknowledged. Spring festivals were the time when Greek theatre came into its own. There were competitions to name the foremost poets/playwrights who tended to specialise in either comedy or tragedy. The events were attended by people from every walk of life, and became a platform for philosophy and politics. Aristotle wrote on both topics but is renowned in the world of drama for his definition of the elements of good tragedy in his treatise on *Poetics*, in which he emphasised a state of extreme emotional expression which he labelled *catharsis*. His use of a medical term which meant ridding the body of unwanted elements – in this case emotions – associated the art of medicine with the art of theatre. In so doing he created a structure for the development of drama as therapy. His premise was that identification with the characters portrayed on stage allowed the audience to express pent up feelings of joy, sorrow, anger and fear, resulting in a sense of 'cleansing' the emotions (Buckley, 1992: 11). Aristotle also commented on the theatrical mirroring of life events when he wrote 'certain persons call their work *dramas*, because they *imitate* those who are engaged in *doing* something' (Buckley, 1992: 5). Aristotle maintained that tragedy should give rise to pity for the plight of the hero and fear that such events could happen to oneself in reality (Butcher, 1923: 302).

The concept of catharsis as emotional relief has occupied a central role in the therapeutic use of drama but equally important is the notion that vicarious involvement, identification and the ambivalence of knowing that events on stage are not real, but are perceived to be real *at the moment* result in a temporary suspension of disbelief. This is an act in which both audience and actors willingly participate and collude to create effective theatre. The tenet of 'as if' is central to dramatherapy – allowing belief and disbelief to be present simultaneously.

## *The relevance of the evolution of drama to dramatherapy*

The principles of dramatherapy, including play, movement, ritual, action, metaphor, distance, catharsis, group involvement, actor and audience, and exploration are all contained within the fabric of drama as it developed chronologically. An outline of their evolution is described below.

- Play – a basic element of dramatherapy. Slade describes play as 'a form of expression that concerns the whole nature of man and woman' (1995: 15). Whilst children's play is accepted as part of their development, play is often seen as unbefitting to adult life.

The ability to play spontaneously is frequently lost and play is usually structured into organised games and/or sports with rules and an element of competition. Any spontaneous play tends to be role play when one person either mimics another, or takes on roles in a light-hearted fashion. An emphasis on adult play is made by Blatner and Blatner (1988a: 33) when they maintain that play is a medium for learning in adulthood as well as childhood, increasing creative ability and providing a context for self-expression in which otherwise unacceptable behaviour can be tolerated. Children play with toys as if they were real, dolls and teddies are given personalities, cars are 'driven' as if they were real, imaginary liquids are 'drunk' from imaginary cups. Later children play at being other people and 'become' (for example) father going to work or the nurse giving an injection. This is called 'imitative play' and is a way of discovering roles, learning about others, coming to terms with unpleasant situations, such as having an injection, and reliving pleasant ones, such as a picnic. Imagination is crucial for creativity, self-awareness, problem-solving and understanding others, and is basic to drama. The element of play in dramatherapy allows a distancing from reality and makes the process enjoyable. It is perhaps relevant to point out here that, in some forms at least, playtherapy *per se* relates strongly to dramatherapy.

- Movement – early rituals were a method of communication in which body movement, dance and sound predominated. Dramatherapy is invaluable in the treatment and care of people who are either non-verbal, or who find oral expression difficult. Personal expression through movement and dance provide a medium for release of tension, telling a story, or communicating feelings without words. In this respect dramatherapy shares something with dance movement therapy (for an account of which see Meekums, 2002).

- Ritual – the theory that early rituals developed from adult play is credible because play is an integral element of drama. Ritual is an important element in dramatherapy. Repetition of sounds, movements and words are useful for creating boundaries and providing a secure working environment. Transitional rituals (rites of passage), for example those of birth, marriage and mourning, are an integral part of everyday life, and assist in the expression and control of emotions. In therapy, they can equally support individuals and groups in the process of meeting, parting and change.

- Action – drama is action, 'a thing done'. Unlike the 'talking therapies', conflicts and problems can be approached through metaphorical representation. By enacting an unfamiliar role it is possible to experience new ways of being. Exploring a familiar role facilitates the discovery of a new perspective on life. Here (and elsewhere), the relationship of dramatherapy to psychodrama of which 'action' is a central element is apparent (see Wilkins, 1999).
- Metaphor – drama is essentially an art form which allows metaphorical expression of strong emotion. Although the therapeutic value lies in the dramatic process, it is important to acknowledge the artistic component inherent in drama. Spontaneity and creativity are essential ingredients, and there is a therapeutic satisfaction in knowing that the work is valued.
- Distance – theatre allows the spectators to distance themselves from the action. They know that events taking place on stage are an imitation of reality, but are involved cognitively and emotionally 'as if' they were real. Identification with a character whose situation, feelings and/or personality are akin to one's own allows a detachment that reality does not. It is easier and safer to comment on the character first, before acknowledging any similarity with self. 'Therapeutic distance' is an essential element of dramatherapy.
- Catharsis – the word *catharsis* as well as being a medical term, was commonly associated with spiritual purification and in mythology with rebirth and metamorphosis (Nichols and Zax, 1977: 2). So there is an affiliation to the spiritual world of the psyche and the notion of transformation. The word catharsis, in the sense of emotional release, was used by Bruer and Freud in the early days of psychoanalysis and has been adopted by other psychotherapists to become a common feature in the description of the psychotherapeutic process although it has a variety of meanings (Nichols and Zax, 1977: 1). Just as theatre allows for the expression and release of feelings, so does dramatherapy.
- Group involvement – drama was originally an important part of community life. Similarly, dramatherapy is essentially a collective activity, in which group members co-operate and support each other in a shared activity. All the components of group therapy are present within the framework of a creative experience. These components include: interactions between different individuals with different experiences; self-disclosure and supportive feedback; development of trust through shared experiences; the

acceptance and support of peers; and taking 'risks' in a safe setting.

- Actor and audience – as theatre evolved from a group action when Thespis stepped out from the chorus, so, as well as being a group approach to therapy, dramatherapy has been developed to encompass therapy on an individual basis, with the therapist acting as the audience or witness to the action. All the elements of drama are present, but the 'community' is limited to the client and therapist alone. Both group and individual methods have their place in the overall therapeutic milieu.

- Exploration – Aristotle wrote influential theses on both philosophy and politics. Whilst his work was aimed at society in general, dramatherapy deals with these topics on a personal level. Clients are supported in the exploration and formation of their own philosophy of life, and personal power struggles. The search for identity and fulfilment is facilitated by engagement in the dramatic process. It is individuals who make their own inquiry to form an opinion without influence from the therapist. Any attempt to influence other's ideas through the medium of drama is the province of commercial theatre, not dramatherapy.

## The development of drama as therapy

Rhythms and dances used in early religious rituals were capable of creating a trance-like state in which it was considered possible to communicate with the gods (Sargant, 1957: 88). In time the role of Shaman, a religious, magical person, came into being. The Shaman became an intermediary with the gods and the invoked trance was the means of contact. It is a small step from contacting gods to assuming their magical powers, and in time the Shaman became a healer of body, mind and spirit. Ritual became associated with healing and altered states of consciousness as a means of restoration. Shamanism is still practised today in many cultures, including those of Native America and Australia (Drury, 1989: 11–22). In Sri Lanka the shamanic healing session is a public ritual in which the community is involved as an audience in a trance-induced drama akin to a theatrical event (Casson, 1984: 18).

Although it is accepted that the Shaman evolved from ancient ritual practices (Drury, 1989: 2), it was not until the eighteenth century that drama began to make an impact on the treatment of the mentally ill. Then theatre became acceptable as a form of recreation for the mentally disturbed. Later, participation in drama was seen as therapeutic, and stages were commonly introduced to mental hospitals (Jones, 1996: 47). Plays were written by and for the inmates, probably the most well-known being by the Marquis de Sade who was himself a patient in Charentan Hospital in Paris. Some productions were open to the public in a manner that would not be considered appropriate today as the productions were seen as an opportunity to make the mentally ill the object of fun and derision. Nevertheless the seeds for the development of therapeutic theatre were being sown.

## Connections between theatre and therapy

There were three people who made a large contribution to theatre as therapy in the early twentieth century and who were thus an influence on the developers of dramatherapy (Jones, 1996: 54).

- Nikolai Evreinov was a Russian theatre director who linked theatre and therapy in his account of 'Theatrotherapy' written in 1927. He emphasised the process experienced by the actors, rather than the performance. This concept is fundamental to dramatherapy today. Evreinov saw theatre as a form of therapy for actors and a means of 'stage management' for life. He also linked theatre and play as important to the development of intelligence (Jones, 1996: 55).
- Vladimir Iljne was also Russian, but was forced to leave his country for political reasons, and settled in Paris in the 1920s. On a journey to Hungary, he came upon Ferenczi who was using role play in a psychoanalytic context. This inspired Iljne to develop 'Therapeutic Theatre'. He worked with groups or individuals using drama games and improvisation (Jones, 1996: 58).
- Jacob Levi Moreno was born in Romania, but his parents moved to Austria when he was a child. He studied medicine and philosophy in Vienna, and worked as a doctor there. Moreno was interested in theatre but was dissatisfied with the contemporary manner in which plays were produced (Hare and Hare, 1996: 7). He created his own improvised 'Theatre of Spontaneity', based on real-life stories rather than fiction. Finding the method brought about changes in the actor he proceeded to forge a link between theatre and therapy. Moreno moved to America in 1927, where he continued his work developing a theatrical structure as a

basis for a therapeutic method he called 'Psychodrama' (Marineau, 1989: 93/4). An introduction to psychodrama can be found in Wilkins (1999), a companion volume to this one.

Therapeutic theatre blossomed in the late nineteenth and early twentieth centuries, an era when theatre itself was experiencing radical developments. This blossoming too was important to the development of dramatherapy. Directors and playwrights whose influence is particularly relevant to dramatherapy are:

- Constantin Stanislavski, a theatre director who is considered to have been most influential in effecting change in the evolution of theatre at that time (Roose-Evans, 1970: 7). He disliked the conventional star system and instituted an ensemble style of acting which was further developed by Brecht, Grotowski and Boal, described below. At the Moscow Arts Theatre, Stanislavski established spontaneous performance or *improvisation* in rehearsal as a vehicle to aid actors in their preparation for performance. He maintained that acting was not imposed from the outside – putting on an act – but came from within the actor and had a spiritual element (Stanislavski, 1987: 49). His technique was designed to evoke memories which stimulate the required emotion for the action portrayed on stage. By associating real situations with the character and exploring those feelings in improvisation, the actor is able to reproduce actual emotional responses. About this time Moreno began using similar techniques to explore real life situations and based his method of psychodrama on improvisation.
- Bertholt Brecht introduced his method of 'alienation' in theatre in the 1930s. His aim was to remind the audience at times that the happenings on stage were not real in order to draw attention to an issue. He wrote and produced plays such as *The Caucasian Chalk Circle, Mother Courage* and *The Threepenny Opera* with an unrealistic plot or a strong political theme aiming to bring spectators face-to-face with reality. The intention was not just to entertain, but to arouse awareness of political injustice.
- Antonin Artaud, a French director in the 1930s, wanted the audience to identify with the action on stage to a point where they were confronted by their own lives and inner conflicts. This he termed the 'Theatre of Cruelty' (Braun, 1982: 182). Artaud felt that theatre should enable the spectator to find a different

perception of life (Artaud, 1970: 70), and hoped to move away from text and realism to become more spiritual – almost a holy place (Jones, 1996: 247).

After the Second World War, the development of theatre continued and, as previously, these developments were linked to 'theatre as therapy' and as such a further influence on dramatherapy. Significant figures from this time include:

- Jerzy Grotowski, a Polish theatre director who, in the 1960s, aimed to discard the grand trappings of theatre. He considered the actor–audience relationship as the focus of theatre. The stage was important only as far as it assisted that relationship. In Grotowski's work, stage was variable, the actors sometimes performing in the round, or mingling with the audience, or distanced from them (Grotowski, 1968: 20). He regarded the actors as central to the performance and the use of their bodies rather than script as a means of communication. In order to develop non-verbal expression, he encouraged physical exercises and ritual as a means of actor preparation. Eventually, Grotowski discarded conventional theatre for a communal exploration using ritual and movement so developing his 'paratheatrical' mode of working (Braun, 1982: 200).
- Augusto Boal, a Brazilian theatre director, who was affected by the political oppression in the 1970s. He perceived theatre as a possible medium to effect reform. Through theatre, Boal aimed to bring an awareness of both the oppressive situation and the possibility of change. He developed his political *Theatre of the Oppressed* in the form of Arena Theatre in which the audience is asked to express comments or intervene in the power issues being represented on stage (Boal, 1979: 180).

## The beginnings of dramatherapy

The term dramatherapy was first used in the UK by Peter Slade. This was in a paper he gave to the British Medical Association in the late 1930s (Langley, 1995/6) and was the first contemporary recognition of the healing properties of drama and a record of his work at the time. Slade became interested in children's play when he was a young actor and realised that drama originated in play. He later worked with children in an Arts Centre and in education. Slade went on to develop his method in adult mental health by collaborating with a Jungian analyst, Dr Kraemer. It was during this period that he was invited to speak to the British Medical Association and the term 'dramatherapy' was born. However, drama had been used as a medium for healing for centuries and Slade does not see himself as the originator of dramatherapy but as part of its evolution. Nevertheless, his innovative work was a landmark in the therapeutic journey – he devoted over 60 years of his professional life to proving the importance of drama to the processes of healing and growth. His work is recorded in his collected papers (the Peter Slade Collection) which are held by the John Rylands University Library in Manchester.

Although Slade was the first person to use the term 'dramatherapy' (Jones (1996: 44) records that one of the earliest uses of 'Drama Therapy' in the USA was by Florsheim in 1946), the dramatic form has been applied to the process of healing since antiquity. However, many authorities trace the emergence of drama as therapy in modern western culture to continental Europe in the nineteenth century (see the British Association of Dramatherapists' website – www. badth.org.uk). At this time, the function of 'catharsis' was being explored in the literature and theatres were built in psychiatric hospitals in France and Germany expressedly for treating patients. Later, there were important developments in Russia where Iljne developed 'therapeutic theatre' and Evreinov advanced his notion of 'theatrotherapy' as 'a way of working [which] encouraged the exploration of the internal and psychological process involved in acting, rather than an emphasis on performance' (British Association of Dramatherapists' website).

## The task of dramatherapy

The main task of the dramatherapist is to facilitate the client's progress through an appropriate dramatic experience that will allow healing to take place. In order to do this, the therapist and client must first form a relationship that enables them to work together towards this end. Dramatherapists must provide a secure space and select an appropriate dramatic medium and structure. Ideally the client contributes to this selection process. Dramatherapists act as supports and guides throughout the therapy. As therapy inevitably evokes emotional reactions, they will also supply strategies enabling the containment of feelings that are aroused during the process.

Dramatherapy utilises all the aspects of drama that are potentially healing. Probably the best known is *catharsis*, or the expression of deeply felt emotion, but equally important is the ability to distance oneself from personal issues. There is a sense of the situation being real, because it is happening now, but also unreal because the events that are happening are 'make believe' in the manner of play. The creativity of drama is used to gain a greater understanding of self, as unconscious feelings, thoughts and issues come to the surface and are expressed through metaphor (Grainger, 1995: 12). The strengthened capacity for creativity is also an aid to problem solving.

As well as being a powerful agent for personal therapeutic change, drama is also a powerful tool to effect social or political awareness and the two modes should not be confused. Theatre has been used to highlight issues of power and injustice for centuries, from the days of Aristotle, through the middle ages up to the present time. The playwright John Skelton is reputed to have criticised the young King Henry VIII personally through theatre. At the same time writers of morality plays attempted to raise issues concerning the church and its teaching (Styan, 1996: 68–73). More recently playwrights such as Ibsen, Brecht and Beckett have presented social and political issues (Hartnoll, 1985: 214, 255, 261). In the 1930s Jacob Moreno initiated the 'Living Newspaper' which explored current topics, and also 'sociodrama' which differed from social drama in that it encouraged members of the audience to take on roles influencing social themes. Sociodrama is still in use as a method of exploring and treating social problems today. More recently, Augusto Boal created his own method of audience involvement, which he calls 'Theatre of the Oppressed' and in which the intention is to enhance political awareness and bring about social change (Boal, 1994: 26). He includes the audience in the action and invites them onto the stage to demonstrate alternative ways of dealing with the situation being explored by taking on roles within the drama, thus expressing other opinions.

## The development of dramatherapy in the UK

Dramatherapy was evolving at a time when theatre itself was developing vigorously (see above). During that period contemporary thought, ideals and techniques put drama in the spotlight. The mid twentieth century was a period when educationalists began to see the value of drama for its own sake and not just as a way of learning Shakespeare. For example, Dorothy Heathcote was using drama creatively with disadvantaged people and Veronica Sherborne was using movement with physically and mentally disabled children. Among practitioners of theatre and drama, there was a general move towards personal development and the therapeutic mode. Some of the major innovators were:

- Peter Slade, at that point an actor, was employed at an Arts Centre in the 1930s. He found that when using improvisation and drama exercises in rehearsals with his actors not only did their performance improve, but they also gained in confidence. Slade started drama classes for the children who attended the Centre, and realised the potential for change, as behaviour began to improve. As his reputation grew, he moved in both educational and therapeutic circles, at one time working with a Jungian psychotherapist (Langley, 1995/6). In 1954 he published *Child Drama* which was an account of his work and philosophy which became essential reading for drama teachers.
- (Marion) Billy Lindkvist, was a member of the Religious Drama Society in London in the 1960s. She had a dream that she was performing in a hospital alongside patients who were participating with her. She was inspired to act upon her dream, and a group of actors, both amateur and professional, began visiting hospitals with improvised theatre which encouraged audience involvement. The group was called KATS and organised short training courses for others under the name SESAME (Jones, 1996: 87). Billy Lindkvist used a method of working based on movement and drama which later became known as the 'Sesame Method' which is described in detail by Jenny Pearson (1996).
- Sue Jennings, when a young drama student, was asked by a local hospital doctor to work with patients in a mental hospital during her long vacation. Later as an actress, she was to put this experience to good use when she worked in a school for children with disabilities. She found that the children who were most disruptive were sent to her drama classes and began to show some change in behaviour. She later worked with Gordon Wiseman to create the Remedial Drama Centre in London. Like Slade in the 1930s they were not working as teachers in school, but as social

educators facilitating self-awareness with a view to behavioural modification. Sue Jennings has written widely on dramatherapy and many of her books are listed in the chapter on *Suggested Further Reading*. She has also established a website designed to be a resource for dramatherapists across the world. The early work Sue Jennings did with children coincided with the time Billy Lindkvist created Sesame, although they were not known to each other at that time.

Apart from the people already mentioned, there were many others, working in hospitals and special schools who were developing dramatherapy independently and unknown to each other. They worked in their own way, coming from a variety of professional backgrounds and diverse theoretical principles, but all moving towards the same end, that is, to what has become known as *dramatherapy*.

## The development of dramatherapy as a profession

As interest in dramatherapy grew so did the need for an exchange of ideas between those who were already practising, and training for other interested professionals. As development was so isolated, the desire for exchange of ideas increased. Partly in response to this need, the British Association of Dramatherapists (BADth) was formed in 1976, and it was under its auspices that the training courses developed – each keeping its own identity but working to a core curriculum. Previously, commencing with short courses, a pattern of training had begun to evolve, until eventually two-year part-time courses were introduced. In 1977, Sue Jennings established a course at Hertfordshire School of Art and Design (now the University of Hertfordshire) and a second course was founded at The College of Ripon and York St John in 1978 (Meldrum, 1994: 13), which was later validated by the University of Leeds. Meanwhile, Billy Lindkvist established a one-year full-time course for Sesame which later moved to the (then) London School of Speech and Drama. In the early 1970s, Sesame KATS group had run a series of weekend workshops for a group of psychiatric hospitals in the Exeter area. Devon County Drama Organisers and later South Devon College Drama Department ran short in-service courses designed to meet the further needs of participating members of staff. In 1980 a two-year Postgraduate Diploma course was introduced at South Devon College. This was similar to those in Hertfordshire and York. Later the course was validated by the University of Exeter to comply with the policy of the British Association of Dramatherapists, and in line with the other courses which were by that time also university-validated postgraduate diplomas. The University of Plymouth later became the validating body. In 1995 additional courses were validated in Manchester and Edinburgh.

Initially, Sesame (validated by The Open University) resisted the notion of dramatherapy and did not fuse with the Association until later (Jones, 1996: 88). As all courses became validated by universities and the profession became established, there was an increased desire for research. The qualifying courses in dramatherapy are now a degree of Master of Arts in Dramatherapy.

As the number of practising dramatherapists increased, the Association, which was originally formed for the mutual support of its members, became a means of professional development. In 1990, a salary scale was approved by the Whitely Council, which regulated salaries and conditions in the UK National Health Service (NHS). This enabled the employment of dramatherapists in NHS establishments. Professional negotiations did not stop there. In the mid 1990s the British Association of Dramatherapists joined with the Art and Music Therapy Associations and together were accepted by the Council for Professions Supplementary to Medicine (CPSM). After a long period of negotiating, the three Arts Therapies finally became State Registered in 1998. Now Arts Therapist (Drama) is a protected title and nobody can call themselves a Dramatherapist unless they are registered with the Health Professions Council (HPC) which is now the UK regulator of health care professions (see below).

## *The British Association of Dramatherapists*

The British Association of Dramatherapists (BADth) has moved from being a small group of people with a diversity of backgrounds to become a formal, recognised and dynamic body of professionals and is now the professional organisation for dramatherapy in the UK. Since its inception the Association has developed from a support group for a few people experimenting with drama as therapy, to an internationally recognised organisation with:

- A register of members who agree to comply with a code of practice
- An elected executive committee and officers
- A mechanism to accredit dramatherapy training courses and also training in supervision
- An Annual General Meeting in order to present and hear the views of members and agree policy
- Regular conferences for the exchange of knowledge and ideas
- State recognition and representatives on the Statutory Board of Arts Therapists on the Council for Professions Supplementary to Medicine (CPSM) which was reshaped and renamed as the Health Professionals Council (HPC) in April 2002.

Membership of the association is open to qualified dramatherapists and dramatherapists in training. Associate Membership is open to unqualified but interested people.

Details of the terms and conditions of membership are available from the Association and via its website (www.badth.org.uk) which includes explanations of the theoretical basis for dramatherapy, the history of dramatherapy and much more.

## *Dramatherapy and the Health Professions Council (HPC)*

The co-ordination with Art, Music and Dance Therapists was the result of a prolonged period of dialogue in which they grew closer as a body, and that enabled the organisations to negotiate for State Registration. This registration was by the Health Professions Council which regulates health professions. To quote a statement from the Partner Manual (HPC, 2004), in order 'to protect health and wellbeing of people who use the services of the health professionals it regulates'. As stated above, Arts Therapist is now a protected title. Each discipline still retains an individual Professional Association but they unite in professional negotiations.

Registration as a dramatherapist is dependent upon the successful completion of one of the approved courses leading to a Masters degree (see above). Although each of these courses is different, they have common elements which are:

- Experience and competence in a broad range of drama and theatre skills, approaches and techniques
- Understanding and awareness of relevant psychological, psychotherapeutic and anthropological principles and practices
- Participation in an ongoing, experiential dramatherapy training group
- Knowledge of related therapies such as art, music, dance movement and play therapies
- Supervised dramatherapy practice
- Continuous assessment and written work
- Personal development/personal therapy.

More information about this particular aspect of the profession of dramatherapy including details of entry requirements and pay scales is available from www.nhscareers.nhs.uk.

## The development of dramatherapy outside the UK

Alongside the development of dramatherapy in the United Kingdom, there was a growth in other countries too. Jones (1996: 94) describes this progress. Playtherapy and drama were being used in social work and education as early as the 1940s and 1950s in the Netherlands and in 1978 an arts therapy course with a specialism in dramatherapy was offered at the Hogeschool, Nijmegen. In the USA, short courses in Drama Therapy were offered in 1971 at Turtle Bay Music School in New York City. In 1979, the United States' National Association for Drama Therapy came into being and Drama Therapy courses were developed. During the 1980s and 1990s, training has been established in India, Israel, Portugal, Germany, Ireland, Jamaica and Norway (Jones, 1996: 94).

There is now a strong body of Arts Therapists in Europe who formed the European Consortium of Arts Therapies Training and Education (ECArTE) in 1991 (ECArTE, 1999). ECArTE holds annual meetings to discuss training issues, share ideas and to encourage students and staff to exchange with their peers in other countries. Therapists from a variety of countries across the world meet at the ECArTE biannual conference. The proceedings of these conferences are published and available for general purchase.

# 2

# THEORY INTO PRACTICE

Play is the basis of dramatic activity; in it one willingly enters a state of make-believe. In doing so, one enters a reality for the moment of the existence of the play, creating a tension between make-believe and truth. The capacity to play is a natural feature of childhood and is described in detail in the book on playtherapy, by Di Gammage, to be published later in this series. Play may be understood as characterised in three developmental stages. At first children's play is exploratory, using senses, voice and movement. It is then extended to involve objects which later become the focus for the projection of personalities or special features. This is symbolic play which paves the way for rituals which may become established as important, for example, the routine of preparing for bedtime or going to nursery school. At a later stage children enter into role play with make-believe characters such as knights in armour or builders on a construction site. As the capacity for play develops, other art forms (for example, dance, drama, art) become involved. Jones (1996: 171) lists the important areas of play in dramatherapy. These are:

- Play as a way of learning about and exploring reality
- Play as a special state with particular relationships to time, space and everyday rules and boundaries
- Play having a symbolic relationship in relation to an individual's life experiences
- Play as a means of dealing with difficult or traumatic experiences
- Play's relationship to an individual's cognitive, social and emotional development
- Play's connection to drama as part of a developmental continuum.

Blatner and Blatner (1988a: 10) point out that '(play) is not done for the purposes of performing for an audience or for competition'. This is an important point: play is entered into for its own sake, the very experience being the vital factor. Performance comes at a later date, when a child wishes to communicate a story in the form of a presentation. Wilshire (1982: 108) says that 'theatre is play which is earnest', linking the two. He also quotes Bradley as saying that 'play need not involve make-believe'. Play can be based on reality. Dramatherapy incorporates both make-believe and real theatre. The steady unbroken development of drama from play through to theatre is parallel to the development of children's play.

In order to utilise its potential, it is helpful to regard drama as consisting of a number of components of a process which starts with a baby's play. As they grow, children experiment with movement and voice. This is followed by symbolic play with toys, experiments with movement to music, rituals such as those used at bedtime which often include storytelling and finally to pretence, for example to 'be' father, teacher, workman or another real person. This can lead to impromptu scenes and play-acting. In drama we move through a similar process of: Play–Movement–Voice–Symbolic play (puppets, toys, etc.)–Dance–Ritual–Storytelling–Role play–Improvisation–Scripted plays–Theatre.

Any of these, severally, sequentially or together, can be utilised in a dramatherapy session regardless of its place in the order of the process. There is no rigid separation but a merging as some elements overlap others. The elements of the list vary in character from free expression to strictly structured work.

During their training, dramatherapists gain practical experience of the whole sequence of theatre art as well as acquiring therapeutic understanding. This equips them to select the form of dramatic intervention appropriate for a particular group or individual at a particular time. There are as many ways of working as there are dramatherapists, each of whom create their own method which may vary according to circumstances and with client needs.

## Theoretical foundations

Like other creative therapies, dramatherapy is not underpinned by any one particular psychological theory. It is possible, for example, to be a 'psychodynamic' dramatherapist paying heed to processes such as transference and defence mechanisms or to be more 'humanistic' emphasising the client's experience in the 'here and now'. In practice, dramatherapists may be informed by any one or more of a number of theories, these in turn influence their work. For example:

- Jungian psychology (Dekker, 1996: 39) is the main basis for the Sesame Course
- Psychoanalysis – specifically Winnicott's concepts of potential space and the transitional object, and also theories of Melanie Klein inform work with script (Jenkyns, 1996: 26)
- Emunah finds that humanistic psychology with its emphasis on the creative self provides an appropriate dramatherapeutic framework (Emunah, 1994: 26)
- Work with children is influenced by Erikson and Klein's theories of development (Bannister, 1997: 23)
- Sociological theory incorporating concepts of Goffman, Mead and Buber give a clear understanding of role, and are themselves derived from theatre (Landy, 1986: 79)
- Family therapists work dramatherapeutically using Systems theory (Shuttleworth, 1987: 124).

## Dramatherapy techniques

Dramatherapy is a creative approach to therapy and growth in many senses. It draws on a repertoire of theatre skills and practices as well as the even older traditions such as storytelling and play. These all depend on creativity – the innate creativity of all human beings and the creatively applied skills of trained dramatherapists. They use knowledge from training and experience, in conjunction with their professional judgement, to respond to the needs of groups and individuals. As acknowledged above, the real essence of dramatherapy is the drama itself, but within it there are exercises and procedures that help to focus on and explore the elected topic. Some of the techniques at the disposal of the dramatherapist are:

- Games – including children's games, team games and those specifically designed to assist actors in stagecraft
- Exercises – created for a specific purpose such as to develop skills, create confidence and trust in individuals and groups, often specifically designed for the training of actors

- Improvisation – the spontaneous enactment of a scenario or story without prior rehearsal
- Rehearsed scenes or stories – these may themselves be developed by groups and therapists working together
- Script – either enactment of a section of a play, a fully rehearsed performance before an audience, or improvisations around the theme of a play or scene
- Storytelling – the recounting of stories to the group, or the creating of a story by the group, sometimes followed by enactment or improvisation around the theme.

Before they focus on the practice of dramatherapy *per se* and decide on the most appropriate device or devices to use, dramatherapists consider both intent and process. The aims of dramatherapists and clients together will depend upon a variety of factors and needs. So it is necessary to ask: 'What is our goal in this group or with this person?'. In broad terms, intention may, for example, be to:

- Improve quality of life providing stimulation, assisting mobility or aiding and encouraging the use of memory when the condition is progressive
- Remedy behaviour – for example, social skills training
- Work on the inner self – the exploration of cognitive, emotional and spiritual conflicts
- Come to terms with irremediable disability (see Langley and Langley, 1983: 17).

Although any dramatherapy technique can be used to work towards any of these goals, games and exercises are more likely to be selected when the objective is to improve quality of life and those techniques which are more concerned with role are probably more appropriate for behavioural and psychotherapeutic exploration.

## *The nine core processes of dramatherapy*

Another approach is to consider the process rather than the method when selecting dramatic techniques. Jones describes nine core processes derived from theatre and suggests they are used as guide for dramatherapy (Jones, 1996: 99). These are:

1 Dramatic projection – the process of selecting aspects of self and using the dramatherapy experience to change one's perception of the situation. An example would be if the client who was having difficulties with his relationship with his mother deliberately took on the role of mother in an improvisation. In the process he may well have an insight into his mother's behaviour which alters his perception of his actual relationship with his mother.

2 Therapeutic performance process – the process of discovering, when taking part in a dramatic action, needs which may not have been previously recognised. By taking on different roles or directing the process of the action the clients get insight into their own personalities. This is made explicit by expressing them to an audience or the therapist.

3 Dramatherapeutic empathy and distancing – the process of playing a character or taking on a role in drama allows clients to identify with that role. The unreality of the drama creates a distance between fact and fiction that facilitates objectivity with respect to own situations.

4 Personification and impersonation – the process of symbolically representing something important through character, role or object such as a puppet or toy. This allows clients to talk freely about the problems the object or role faces when, in fact, they are the client's own.

5 Interactive audience and witnessing – the process of being a spectator and participant simultaneously. There is an element in drama where one can see oneself whilst acting a part. It is important to be able to view oneself as well as to be viewed by the audience. It is also part of the group process to be a witness to others' expression of their own issues.

6 Embodiment – dramatising the body – the process of using the body alone without speech to express feelings, thoughts and experiences. Physical activity is an intrinsic part of expression. Clients can learn both the lessening of tension and improved expression by movement alone.

7 Playing – the process of understanding through enjoyment and having fun. It has already been stated that the basis of dramatic activity is play and this is an important component. The sense of playfulness can be revealing when clients discover the truthfulness of reality hiding in the playful activity.

8 Life-drama connection – the process of relating drama to real-life events, experiences and beliefs. All drama is based on

reality either explicitly or through metaphor. Clients discover associations with real happenings in their lives and can learn from them by comparison, explanation and discussion.

9  Transformation – the process of change. Objects are used as symbols to represent important articles or events in clients' lives. By involvement in role play in improvisation clients can restructure and adapt situations to their own lives.

Jones' view is particularly appropriate because dramatherapists agree that it is involvement in the process of drama, enabling self-realisation that creates the potential for change in dramatherapy. These nine core processes are present in theatre and Jones shows how they apply to dramatherapy.

## The five stages of dramatherapy

Another approach to process is suggested by Emunah (1994: 34–45). She follows the course of five stages of theatrical development as they relate to dramatherapy. The five stages are:

1  Dramatic play in which a playful environment is created using physically active and interactive games and trust exercises. Simple children's games can produce fun and energy. An example is 'Off Ground Touch' where the group is chased round the room by one of its members, the first person caught becomes the chaser but the other group members can save themselves by getting their feet off the ground before being touched. The cycle repeats for as long as seems appropriate.

2  Scene work develops playful improvisations into structured scenes and creates characters. An example would be an improvisation of a street scene which can be developed by each group member deciding to be a certain character and in pairs agreeing on a scene to be enacted, making the whole into an impromptu play. An example could be that of traffic warden and a motorist, and possibly the issuing of a parking ticket.

3  Role play focuses on real-life roles, allowing the security of dramatic fiction to give group members sufficient distance to consider the actual roles they occupy in their lives. Taking on roles of real life, such as parent, boss at work or the peacemaker, allows clients to consider the roles they have in reality, experiment with new roles and alter existing ones if desired.

4 Culminating enactment examines actual issues and conflicts that exist in the life of individuals. Moving from imaginary situations to events one faces in actuality allows clients to explore their own issues 'as if' they were happening at the present time and to make realistic adjustments if they so choose.

5 Dramatic ritual often created by the group members themselves, to lead from the intense introspection back to everyday routine. It is important for group members to leave the dramatherapy session ready to move to their next activity. Some form of ritual such as forming a circle and making a statement of their next activity, or stating their name and how they are feeling, helps people to return to reality and everyday life.

Not all groups go through all five stages. Again, there is scope for the dramatherapist to adapt the progression according to the implicit or explicit needs of the group. For example, particularly vulnerable people may progress from fantasy work to dramatic ritual omitting the personalised role play which may be too intense and intimate for them to cope with at that time.

## Stages of dramatherapy

Regardless of the theoretical understanding of the practitioner, dramatherapy sessions move through common stages. These are:

- Warm-up – the group prepare themselves both physically and mentally for dramatic activity. An active game such as any chasing game in which the group has to move around raises energy levels and stimulates physical senses. An example is 'Tag' where an individual chases the group in hope of catching someone. Anyone who is touched becomes the chaser. A mental warm-up is anything that allows people to forget the day-to-day activities of life and leave the mind free for dramatic activities. An example would be to work in pairs, one having the role of policeman, the other one pedestrian. The policeman is trying to prevent the pedestrian from walking down a road the pedestrian is trying to pass. What is the conversation between them? They have four minutes to persuade each other of the necessity of their task. Who wins?

- Development phase – explorations on a theme using a dramatic form that is appropriate for the group. Depending on the goal of the group, either roles from a character in a book or film, or real life roles are used. The group then decides on a topic and creates a scene around it, either using other group members or the therapist as audience.

- Closure – the group works towards an expression of feeling and a sense of resolution. Finally the company reflect on the session and, if it is appropriate, share their experience with others in the group. This period of reflection is the time when therapy potentially takes place. The clients think about the meaning of their drama and how it applies to their own reality.

Within this universal framework, there are diverse ways of understanding or describing what happens in dramatherapy. These may be thought of as different models. The structuring of dramatherapeutic work can be helped by considering the various models which have been arrived at by practitioners as they developed their own methods. A model is essentially descriptive of a certain course of action. It is important to understand that the following examples are ways in which some people work, and are intended for guidance and not strict adherence.

## Models of dramatherapy

### The developmental model

The developmental model of dramatherapy assumes a correspondence between what happens in dramatherapy and the way children learn to play. Children's play evolves through three developmental stages which Jennings (1990: 10) terms embodiment/projection/role play or EPR:

- Embodiment play – exploratory play where a child uses his/her senses, mainly of touch and sound, to investigate the immediate environment by such games as banging with a spoon, splashing water and digging in sand.
- Projective play – toys and objects become important and the child becomes attached to his/her favourites. Later toys and objects are used in games to represent people and characters – this is the commencement of symbolic thought (finding a symbol to express ones feelings (see Cattanach, 1994c: 17–22).
- Role play – the child first mimics and then enacts a role other than his/herself in play. This is a time of social interaction and learning as children take on roles such as parent, teacher, bus driver in imaginary situations.

Cattanach (1994a: 28) describes the theme of this model as the 'working and re-working of the life stages and changes of individuals and groups'. Jennings (1993) offers a full analysis and charts of EPR.

Developmental psychology emphasises the sequence of the stages people go through during their lifetime. If there is a blockage at one stage, then this can become an issue in that person's life. There can be an impediment at any stage of life, not just in childhood. The dramatherapist using this model aims to find the faulty stage and rework it dramatically to alter the client's perspective. The same system by which children learn through play can be applied with adults in order to explore relationships and life situations. In terms of this model, a dramatherapy session can be structured around three modes:

- Embodiment – exploration of a theme through the senses, movement and voice. This could include dance, active games, breathing exercises, singing games and much more. When being interviewed by Pamela Mond (see Jennings, 1994: 180), Mooli Lahad described embodiment as 'non-verbal movement' whereas he saw enactment as 'verbal movement'.
- Projection – the use of objects, for example, masks, puppets, toys and rituals, to symbolise people, feelings or situations. Jones (1996: 138–9) summarises the basic stages of 'dramatic projection in dramatherapy'. These centre on the externalisation of 'inner conflicts' through the medium of drama thus allowing a changed perspective and alteration of moods and attitudes.
- Role play – the enacting of real or fantasy roles in improvised or scripted scenes.

Dramatherapists encourage clients to explore their own experience of different life stages by using any of these modes they have used in childhood play.

### Judith understands her mother

*The women's group had been discussing the topic of motherhood. Hazel, the dramatherapist, produced a basket of toys and small objects and asked the group to create a pattern of their family relationships. They chose objects they thought made a statement about the important people in their lives and placed them in positions that represented the relationship* (this is called a spectrogram). *Judith selected a Barbie doll to represent her sister, and placed it with its back to the snail that represented herself. She placed a cuddly teddy as her father close to the snail and facing it, and a wooden Russian doll as her mother between the snail and the Barbie doll, sideways to both of them.*

*Hazel asked Judith to speak as if she were each of the objects in turn and make a statement about their current relationship. As father she said 'I am here for you', as sister she said 'I lead a very different life from you and I don't think you understand me'. As mother she said 'I try to keep the peace between you and your sister'.*

*Hazel then asked her to produce another spectrogram of the family when Judith was five years old. This time she placed a rag doll as herself with a china doll as her sister, they were side by side and the sister said 'We do everything together. I especially enjoy our dancing classes'. Father was still a teddy bear who said 'I am here for you' and mother was a hen who said 'I care for you both and want the best for you'.*

*On reflection, Judith could see how, as a child, she had been jealous of her sister's prettiness and aptitude for dancing. Her mother had tried to help Judith compensate by encouraging her academically, but that had only resulted in Judith despising the person her sister had become. The symbolic representation of the spectrograms had revealed her own misinterpretation of her mother's intentions. She could see how her mother's role had changed from the caring mother hen looking after both chicks to an authoritarian figure keeping them apart lest they hurt each other.*

### The creative-expressive model

This model works on the premise that creativity is one of the healing elements in drama. The emphasis is on the creative act itself, as it happens at the moment. There is no pressure to look into past events or question what is happening or why. The aim is to develop existing skills in the group and generate self-esteem (Cattanach,

1994b: 141). When employing a creative-expressive approach, a range of drama structures are used to stimulate imagination and help clients find their full potential. There may be increased communication and social skills and some insight into problems, but these are not explored in the sessions. It is essentially a non-interpretative way of working (Jennings, 1990: 29).

### Penny struggles for her freedom

*Penny was a member of a dramatherapy group for young people who were substance abusers. Although she had successfully completed treatment, she was reluctant to leave the safety of the hospital because she felt she could not face her friends and relatives. The group was playing energetic games of tag, when Jack, another group member, caught hold of Penny and would not let go. Other group members gathered round and formed a circle. She stopped struggling and said 'I can't get out'. 'You're chicken, why don't you fight?' said Jack. Penny put some real force into her struggle and eventually broke free of the circle. The game finished, so did the session and no further comments were made. A few days later Penny asked the doctor if she could go home for the weekend 'just to see if it's OK'.*

### Integrated model

An integrated model merges two or more models. Jennings (1990: 39) describes an integration of the creative-expressive model with the acquiring of skills or a task-centred model plus the use of psychotherapeutic intervention and interpretation. Following introductory discussion, the group determines its own theme. Selecting from a variety of theatrical and dramatic procedures, the therapist guides the clients through a process that enables them to work on personal issues. These may be matters that involve problem solving, development of skills or self-exploration. Any or all of the modes may be used in any one session.

### The little mermaid's lost voice

*A group began their fourth session by sharing their thoughts and feelings about the last meeting. Jane had left with a sense of unease about the role of 'wicked witch' she had played in the improvisation. David tried to analyse the role in an attempt to help her. Patricia, the therapist, intervened and suggested the group move around the room in a manner which expresses their feelings at the moment. After a time, Patricia suggested the group find a character that fitted the feeling. Jane became the Little Mermaid, deprived of voice, and in the ensuing improvisation was in conflict with David who was in the role of Superman. She resisted his efforts to magically 'make it better' and finally burst into tears. After the action was finished and she was speaking as herself again, she said that her husband had applied for a new job in another part of the country and was expecting her to move with him. She had tried to explain that she was unhappy about the move, but he appeared not to have heard. She felt that, like the Little Mermaid in the story who was unable to speak to the man she loved, she had lost her voice and was not heard by him.*

*Patricia suggested she entered into a role play scene with her husband in which she tried to express herself. Jane found it very difficult to find the words she needed and finally admitted that during this enactment she felt like the wicked witch of last week, destroying someone else's life. Patricia then asked her to reverse roles with her husband, and in doing so, Jane realised her own responses had been inadequate because of her ambivalence about her husband's new work which, although well paid, would involve the upheaval of moving home, leaving friends and family behind.*

During this session the creative-expressive model had paved the way for the task-centred model to help Jane understand her own behaviour.

Another integrated model is described by Chesner (1994a: 61) who contends that as drama is a 'thing done', any activity may be incorporated into the dramatherapy session. Selecting from the whole range of dramatic actions she uses music, dance, puppets, art and storymaking to involve the clients. Her attention is focused on the levels of interaction within the group. These levels are:

- Interaction with the space and objects in it
- Interaction with the therapist or therapeutic team
- Interaction with the peer group.

The mode of action is chosen to enable the exploration of the agreed theme for the session and will vary accordingly.

## The para-theatrical model

Grotowski (see Chapter 1) used ritual, voice and body in his para-theatrical workshops. He disliked the gulf between audience and performer, and developed a form of theatre in which everyone present was involved and the emphasis was on what was happening in the present moment. His techniques have been adapted for dramatherapy and these adaptations are described by Mitchell (1992: 58–67). Using candles to create a ritual perimeter, Mitchell works through seven stages in each session. First the group share their experiences, then they go through a variety of exercises which include movement, voice, exchange of ideas and ending with the use of candles again. The reasoning behind this model is that through shared physical and cognitive actions, clients are prepared to disclose personal and emotional issues in order to effect change, the transition being facilitated by ritual. Of this way of working, Mitchell (1992: 67) states:

> In this approach to dramatherapy, the process of therapy involves enabling clients to devise their own healing rituals. The ritual is not the change itself but the preparation for change ... The para-theatrical model of dramatherapy I believe truly offers dramatherapists an alternative rationale for groupwork which has its roots in the history of theatre and dramatic art.

## The role model

Moreno based his therapeutic theatre on the concept of role. His intention was to focus on the roles people possess and the way they function in them. He believed that successful role function is essential for well-being and psychodrama is concerned with exploring roles, correcting the dysfunctional, expanding the successful and seeking new ones. (See Wilkins (1999), a companion work to this book, for an exploration of psychodrama and the theories and practices of Moreno.)

Building on the concept of role taking and role playing, Landy (1993: 46) has created a dramatherapy role model in which the client works entirely through fantasy roles and their counter-roles, becoming aware of the ambivalent nature of the role and counter-role being present at the same time. He maintains that at the core of his model 'is the notion of paradox, ambivalence and change' (1993: 12). Landy stresses the ambivalence and shows that even in the most extreme commitment to a role it is prominent:

- Within the role itself when competing qualities conflict, as in an attempt to play the fearless hero, when real fears intervened
- Between two conflicting roles as the fearful quality produced the role of the coward
- As an existential state of being and not being, as seeing oneself paradoxically as both hero (not coward) and coward (not hero) at the same time.

The first two elements are similar to Moreno's description of role conflict, but with his emphasis on paradox, Landy has advanced role theory. In Moreno's terms, role reversal in psychodrama allows the protagonist to experience both role and counter-role. Awareness of taking on two paradoxical roles simultaneously creates a tension that can be used therapeutically. Landy sees the healing potential in the stance a person takes in the 'me' and 'not me' paradox of the theatrical and/or therapeutic actor. He maintains that the client is capable of working therapeutically whilst he/she is between the state of 'being' and 'not being' – reality and imagination (Landy, 1993: 46). He says that the client can be truly objective whilst in this 'transitional space' between two realities. Although clients work within an identified role, the process allows a flow in and out of it during the reflection, which guides them to understanding.

Landy describes eight steps that constitute a method of working in role:

1 Invoking the role – getting in touch with the essence of the role to create a character
2 Naming the role – finding an appropriate name for the character
3 Playing out/working through the role – playing the character in a variety of improvised situations
4 Exploring alternative qualities in sub-roles – searching for other aspects of the role not previously considered
5 Reflecting upon the role play – discovering role qualities, functions and styles inherent in the role
6 Relating the fictional role to everyday life
7 Integrating roles to create a functional role system – incorporating the new roles and perception into the role repertoire
8 Social modelling – discovering ways the client's behaviour in role affects others in their social environment.

Using the entire method is long-term work. Landy (1993: 55) does say that his is a method of treatment that need not be followed rigidly, but can be seen as a principle on which to base practice. In an economic climate where brief therapy is encouraged, the whole method may be considered too lengthy and expensive to be practicable. Landy, however, recommends his method for the short-term treatment of selected clients, such as those who have been thrust into a crisis by the death of someone close or by psychological trauma. Exploring roles in depth assists the discovery of other parts of the person which may be helpful. Landy (1996: 196) says of his approach 'Yet paradoxically, as it focuses upon single parts, it points to the possibility of others, alternative personae that can move the person out of a desperate and hopeless condition'.

Using the role model although a powerful way of working, can be less intense than psychodrama, being about fictional roles rather than entering into the real role. Steps 7 and 8 are similar to stages in psychodrama and as a dramatherapeutic technique are steps into real roles.

### Robert finds his strength

*Robert worked on the role he called 'Scaredy-cat'. In improvisations, Scaredy-cat always took the easy option. Whilst exploring the quality of the role, Robert realised that Scaredy-cat was protecting him from dealing with difficult situations. This revealed the 'Protector' within him, a role which he then explored further. Protector was a knight in shining armour, who was ready to defend the weak. The realisation of the potential of the Protector, enabled him to expand that role, finding a resource within himself to balance his fearfulness.*

### The theatrical model
Brenda Meldrum in a personal communication to students, likened the structure and process of a dramatherapy group to a theatrical production. The dramatherapist is seen as an empathic director and the client group the actors. The roles of theatrical director and dramatherapist are compared and contrasted in Table 2.1.

## The importance of 'relationship' in dramatherapy

In this chapter, a variety of methods of dramatherapy have been described, and some psychological theories that assist dramatherapists

Table 2.1   *Roles in theatre and dramatherapy*

| Roles of director | Roles of dramatherapist |
| --- | --- |
| Auditions | Assesses |
| Encourages group cohesion | Encourages group cohesion |
| Facilitates individuals to discover blocks and overcome resistance | Facilitates individuals to discover blocks and overcome resistance |
| Each rehearsal begins with a warm-up | Each session begins with a warm-up |
| Proceeds into active rehearsal | Proceeds into action phase |
| The actors project themselves into the roles they are playing and explore them | Clients use role or other projective means for expression and exploration |
| The actor performs in front of an audience | Clients are observed by each other and/or the dramatherapist |

in their understanding of the process have been indicated. As stated at the beginning of the chapter, there are as many ways of working as there are dramatherapists. Each person experiences drama in their own individual manner. It is essential that both therapist and client find the style of practice that best facilitates exploration, insight and integration for the individual at that moment in time. An attempt to use a model that is unsuitable for the client or uncomfortable for the therapist is a pathway to disaster. What matters in the long run is the *relationship* between therapist and client. It is necessary to develop a working liaison in which the client's needs can be explored within the safe context of dramatic activity. There is no right or wrong way of dramatic enactment – it is the experience that matters. The therapist may act as a container, facilitator and/or participant, but the power to heal is within the client and the process of dramatic action. The dramatherapist has to allow for the individual's interpretation and creativity. It is important, therefore, that the therapist is accepting and non-judgemental of all the client has to offer. Peter Slade gives an excellent example of the way in which he follows and accepts all the images presented by children, providing ideas himself only when the creativity seems to be waning (Slade, 1995: 58).

Unlike psychoanalysis, where the therapist acts as interpreter, or the client-centred model where the therapist responds from their empathic understanding of the client, the dramatherapist, particularly in individual therapy, may participate in the process by taking on a role in the enactment (Johnson, 1992: 113). Clients often arrive with an idea that the therapist will solve all their problems in an unequal relationship of giver and receiver which may be flattering and seductive to the therapist but is counter-therapeutic. It is essential, as far as possible, for the client to be in control of the creative process, with the therapist assisting where necessary. In dramatherapy, the therapeutic relationship is an encounter between two or more people who come together with the mutual intention of therapy as the goal. There must be mutual respect and trust – as Gunzburg (1997: 9) expresses it: 'Therapist and client can only hope to *meet*, never demand or will it of each other.' Dramatherapists may be influenced by a particular psychological theory which will effect the manner in which they work, but they will primarily have a non-judgemental respect for their clients which is pervasive throughout therapy.

# 3

---

# PREPARING FOR DRAMATHERAPY

As the previous chapters indicate, dramatherapy is underpinned by theories as complex and comprehesive as those of any approach to psychotherapy. This theoretical base is a prime consideration when moving towards practice as a dramatherapist. Dramatherapy may be used in a variety of settings (for example, day care facilities, hospitals, schools, private practice) and with a whole range of clients. It may form part of a treatment programme for people who are emotionally or mentally disturbed, people with social or learning difficulties may find it a useful aid to their development, or it may be an agent of personal growth and change. In view of the diverse uses of dramatherapy, there are a number of issues to be considered before the dramatherapist encounters clients in the dramatherapy space. These are considered in this chapter.

## Working with groups or individuals?

One of the first considerations is if group or individual work is indicated (by the needs of the client, and to some extent, the preference of the dramatherapist). Dramatherapists are trained to work with both groups and individuals, facilitating the use of drama towards an increased self-understanding and understanding of society, as well as using it therapeutically in a way that is focused on specific personal issues. Just as dramatherapy has its origins in the rituals performed by people in ancient times (see Chapter 1), and these rituals were initially group activities, so dramatherapy also evolved as a group form. As it became more widespread, so its application as a one-to-one mode of therapy has developed. Dramatherapy with individuals is now an accepted practice. Whether or not there is a need for short-term therapy, difficulties in gathering groups in some areas and the needs of some clients for a one-to-one relationship will determine if dramatherapy is offered on an individual or group basis. The dramatic process is the same for both modes but the difference is that there is only the client and therapist to take on roles, so that there is not the variety of perspectives, concepts and insight for discussion as there is with a group. Dramatherapists have multiple roles. As well as taking on characters (dramatic roles), they are open to being a transference figure (psychological role) and are also the therapist (social role). These are the three main roles mentioned by Johnson (1992: 112). He also lists others and implies that they are emphasised in one-to-one work.

In dramatherapy, as in other approaches, feelings, both positive and negative, and old, unconscious ways of relating, can be projected onto the therapist in what is termed 'transference' (see Jacobs, 1988: 12–15 for a discussion of this term). Although as a psychodynamic concept, transference is not necessarily a part of dramatherapy theory, a brief consideration of its implications for dramatherapy practice and especially how it manifests in individual and group forms may be helpful. This is because (however the phenomenon is understood) whatever is played out in the relationship between client and dramatherapist must be of concern to the latter and dealt with through drama.

Landy (1992: 103–6) considers transference and countertransference in dramatherapy. He points out that transference is a dramatic concept because the client is in effect transforming the actual role of the therapist into a symbolic one (1992: 103) and Jones (1996: 64) takes a similar view. In dramatherapy, since the role play is intrinsic, transference is overt. This is on account of the fact that as Landy indicates (1992: 104), client and therapist cast each other in alternative roles. In this way, in the context of dramatherapy, Landy sees transference as a healthy act, not a neurotic one because transference issues are a legitimate part of drama and may be resolved through it. The dramatherapist needs to be particularly sensitive to the fact that in one-to-one work all transference processes can occur only between client and therapist, then work in such a way as to enable the client to 'work through the spectrum of distance and toward a point of balance' (Landy, 1992: 104). In one-to-one dramatherapy, transference may be worked with by the therapist encouraging the clients to reflect on the enactment to compare the state of being 'in-role' (the world of the imagination) with the state of being 'out-of-role' (the actual world).

Transference issues may arise in dramatherapy groups also, but they are projected onto members of the group as well as the therapist. The group represents society and all its problems and also displays a variety of personalities who each bring their own creativity, ideas and opinions. The lone client does not have this advantage so the dramatherapist then needs to present several points of view. Working with a single client also presents greater possibility of conscious or unconscious collusion – a situation of which dramatherapists must be aware. For example, it is easy for clients who have been the victim of abuse to project the abuser role on to the therapist. Therefore it is also important when taking on a role in one-to-one therapy, to be certain that the dramatherapist is not inadvertently placed in an abusive role.

As pointed out above, most dramatherapists work with individuals or with groups as appropriate for the client. Normally the choice of style will be made on the factors which, in the judgement of the dramatherapist, will result in the most effective therapy but issues such as cost, time and timing, numbers of clients etc. may also influence the choice. Although one-to-one work in dramatherapy is effective and valuable, working as a group can be fun and offers the added therapy of the support and aid that other clients can give. Just as one-to-one work brings the likelihood of particular processes occurring between client and dramatherapist, so, alongside the overt dramatic interactions, dramatherapy groups will be subject to 'group process'. Group process has been variously described (classic descriptions include those of Bion, 1961; Tuckman, 1965; and Rogers, 1970).Whichever modality is chosen, the needs of dramatherapy groups and the responsibilities of the therapist are now considered. One-to-one work follows the same process, so most of the following also applies to it.

## Structuring the dramatherapy session

The first requirement of the dramatherapist is to a build a trusting relationship with the clients. This may take some time with wary clients, but is a necessary basis for therapy. Dramatherapists, if possible in co-operation with the client, have to take several decisions before treatment can commence, for example, whether to work in a group, or to work one-to-one. This will depend on the availability of an appropriate group, the readiness of the client to work with others and the nature of the issues to be confronted. Whichever mode of treatment is decided upon, there are a number of necessary conditions and preconditions which shape the environment in which dramatherapy can be effectively and safely delivered. Some of these are defined by the general needs of treatment and psychotherapy (particularly in health care settings). Some are basic ground rules for psychotherapy of any kind, some are especially relevant to dramatherapy.

### The working environment for dramatherapy

Before client and therapist can work together dramatherapeutically, there are a number of issues to be addressed. These are to ensure that the clients know what will happen, what will ensure their personal safety and that they consent to the process as a whole.

CONSENT    That a client consents to receive the treatment offered to him is necessary on both ethical and legal grounds. Ethically, after the proposed treatment is explained in broad terms his valid autonomous wishes must be respected. Civil law in the UK also mandates that to treat a client, either physically or psychologically, without his consent is a civil wrong. Consent to treatment must be based upon an explanation in terms that the patient is best able to understand, and should include information on: any major hazards, the foreseeable consequences of deciding one way or another, or of not deciding. The explanations given and the client's responses should be recorded in the case notes.

Problems arise when clients are incapable of making the relevant decisions (about each specific treatment) and need, in their best interests, for that treatment to be provided. The refusal and compulsory administration of treatment, in the presence of mental disorder, is dealt with under the Mental Health Act 1983. There is however a much wider group of clients, mostly those suffering from learning difficulties or age-related mental problems who, while not openly refusing treatment, are incapable of understanding what is required, and are therefore incapacitated in terms of consenting. In the UK no other person, including relatives, is empowered to give 'proxy' consent. In these circumstances no patient should be deprived of treatment so the present law permits a therapist to proceed by acting in the patient's 'best interests', defined to include complying with his past expressed wishes and his broad welfare as well as just strict medical considerations. In these circumstances discussion with near relatives may be wise but their views are not legally binding. The issues of the authority to treat incapacitated patients, and the safeguards necessary for this vulnerable group have, in recent years, been much debated in the UK (*Who Decides*, 1997) culminating in the Mental Capacity Act 2005. At the time of writing, the provisions under the Act have not been implemented, but when they are they will: set criteria for incapacity, make provision for Lasting Powers of Attorney to include medical treatment, formalise advance directives about future treatment desires, provide for advocacy services and provide for the therapist to take into account the views of nominated persons or carers. Responsibility for taking appropriate steps to obtain consent or proceed in its absence lies with the individual therapist and is specific to each individual treatment decision. Delay in implementing these generally welcomed measures is due to the need to write a Code of Practice and train appropriate personnel.

In the UK the Mental Health Act is also under review and this means that, important as these two acts are to the safeguarding of both clients and therapist, they are, in the UK, both in a state of flux that make more detailed advice inappropriate in this context. Beyond the above general orientation, therapists are advised to attend to developments within their own field of practice!

A simple description of the content of the session should help to allay anxieties and promote acceptance. Each new activity must be introduced in a clear manner, taking one step at a time. A long string of instructions is confusing to people who may be anxious.

- Any queries must be answered before the session commences.
- Clients are free to question anything at any time and can expect a reasonable reply.
- Clients must be informed that they have the power to withdraw consent at any time.

Parents may consent for minors, but in certain circumstances, if they are thought to fully understand the issues at stake, children can give their own consent. This can be a controversial area and therapists are advised to take local advice from managers or legal advisors.

A helpful pamphlet (*Making Decisions*, 2003) that explains these issues in greater depth is published in the UK by The Lord Chancellor's Office. When working in some other countries, therapists confirm with their professional bodies, the standards by which consent is judged and the appropriate actions if it is absent in that country, before proceeding with treatment.

### Reassuring May

*May was a consenting member of a group of elderly patients. She was upset when the dramatherapist suggested the group play a game from childhood. 'I didn't come here to be treated like a child' she said. The dramatherapist stopped the game and pointed out the object of the exercise. The group was working together, socialising and exercising physically in their attempts to play with a balloon. When she realised that she was not being made to look childish, May joined the game with much energy and enjoyment.*

Physical and emotional problems may cause some people to find dramatic engagement difficult. It is good practice to advise clients that they do not have to participate in any activities if they do not want to – they can just opt out of the exercise and sit at the side until it is finished. Also, to facilitate informed consent, it is useful to have one or two preliminary sessions for newcomers, who can then decide if they wish to continue with dramatherapy.

### Mabel weaves it together

*Mabel was referred to a dramatherapy reality orientation group for people with early dementia. She said that she did not want to join the group, but would do her knitting and watch the others. The dramatherapist asked the group if they were happy with the arrangement and everyone agreed Mabel should stay and do her knitting. The first topic of the day was 'What day is it?' Mabel was the first person with the correct answer. Each time a question was posed she was ready with an answer – usually the correct one. When the dramatherapist asked group members to find a partner and comment on the colour of their dress, Mabel did not move but called across the room 'Ivy's wearing a red cardigan'. When the dramatherapist suggested looking through the window to see what the gardener was doing, Mabel was the first to arrive. She repeated this behaviour for the remainder of the ten sessions, always insisting she was just doing her knitting and watching, but actually becoming a vital and popular group member. If the dramatherapist had insisted that Mabel should not be allowed to become a spectator, both Mabel, the other group members and the dramatherapist would have missed out on some valuable and enjoyable interaction.*

CONFIDENTIALITY    An essential element of a therapeutic relationship is confidentiality. Clients need to be assured that private information, including third party information, will not be divulged to other persons without their permission. Although it is permissible to recount to others one's own experience, group members must agree that any information or event that happens in the group and which relates to the experience of another or would allow the identification of one or more individuals cannot be discussed other than in the group session. Dramatherapists themselves are also bound by rules of confidentiality and will, for example, undertake that no information will be divulged without written consent of the individual concerned. The only exceptions are grave issues of public concern, such as potential suicide, child sexual abuse or homicidal threats.

In these circumstances dramatherapists have to consider their commitment to report to other professionals. There must be an agreement within multidisciplinary teams or even teams of about how much information regarding clients it is necessary and/or desirable to share. This requires discussion with clients and the staff with whom they are involved and that a clear policy is stated.

When working as part of a team, it is often sufficient to keep co-professionals informed by naming the particular issue or relationship that the client worked on without going into details of the nature of the work. Also, reporting threats of harm does not necessarily mean that the therapists have to disclose confidential material, but they have a duty of care to report it to someone in charge. It is sometimes possible to persuade the client to communicate the necessary information themselves – dramatherapists have their own ways of doing this (see the following case example).

### Will gets a hearing

*A group of young men in a forensic unit were all working on family issues. Will came from a professional family who were unable to come to terms with the offences he had committed in order to fund his drug habit. He became very upset following a simulated interview with his mother, and said that he wished he were dead. Another group member said, 'Is that why you stole a knife from the kitchen this morning?' Will admitted he had intended to harm himself, but lacked the courage at the last minute. The dramatherapist encouraged him to talk about his suicidal thoughts, and suggested he told the Charge Nurse about them. He was reluctant to do this, thinking he would be punished for stealing in the same way his parents had punished him – by being ostracised. The dramatherapist offered to go with him to speak to the Charge Nurse after the group had finished and Will agreed. He was surprised when the Charge Nurse listened sympathetically to the account of his suicidal thoughts, praised him for his courage in confessing to the theft, and arranged an appointment with the doctor immediately.*

There is sometimes a sense of guilt and threat of punishment associated with suicidal or aggressive thoughts. Such feelings are often expressed metaphorically in dramatherapeutic action. Once aware of a client's suicidal inclinations, it is important to take some action, but it is not necessary for the dramatherapist to report it alone. By taking matters into their own hands, any therapist can deprive the client of the opportunity to cope with the situation him/herself. It is respectful both to the client and the therapeutic relationship to be supportive of clients in acknowledging the problem for themselves.

CONTAINMENT It is important to keep all the feelings that are expressed or unexpressed during the session contained within the therapy session. A period of reflection and sharing at the end of a session, working in pairs if clients are not happy talking in a group, and a discussion of the previous session to commence the next is a useful way of making both personal and group feelings known. Failure to do so may result in clients being overwhelmed by their own feelings and possibly absorbing other people's as well. This confusion may result in disturbed behaviour or 'acting out' as it is often termed, both in the group and later.

The metaphorical aspect of drama enables people to distance themselves from reality 'as if' events were happening elsewhere. The therapy session can be seen as a huge container for all the feelings and issues of the group.

### *Tony draws the sword*

*Tony was a young man with a drug problem. His family were supportive and tried to help him. The group, who were all confined to a young offender's unit, decided to improvise the myth of Arthur and his accession to the throne. Tony took on the role of the young Arthur trying to pull the sword from the stone. The knights in the improvisation were supportive and wanted him to be king. They said that if any of them gained the sword, they would still appoint him as king. When it was his turn, they cheered and egged him on. With a great effort he pulled the sword out of the stone and achieved his aim to be king.*

*The group were unhappy on account of their being punished by reduction of television time because someone had misbehaved. They thought it unfair that all should suffer because of one person and were grumbling about it among themselves as they entered the dramatherapy space. At the end of the session, Tony admitted that he realised that he could only deal with his drug problem if he made the effort to do it himself. His parents could not do it for him. His insight led to the realisation of other group members that it was no good complaining amongst themselves. They had to approach the person in charge and confront him with their issue.*

CONTRACT   A clear contract setting out the obligations of the therapist and the clients is essential, and is agreed with the group before treatment commences. A dramatherapy contract will normally include:

- Details of the parameters of confidentiality of therapist, for example, to whom the dramatherapist must report
- Details of confidentiality between clients
- Time and place of the sessions
- Duration of the course, for example, how many sessions may be expected
- If applicable, what the physical boundaries of area to be used are. For example, is the kitchen/office/alcove area part of the therapeutic space?

- Possibility of/limitations on physical proximity and touching
- That there shall be no physical violence
- If violent scenes are to be enacted, only cushions or inanimate objects that cannot harm people will be used to facilitate the action
- That clients are expected to remain in the room. If they feel it necessary to leave for any reason, they should not leave others in suspense, but inform the group (or, if this is too difficult at least the therapist) of their intention and the reason for leaving before they go.

PERSONAL IDENTITY   There is often an unconscious fear of losing identity in a group, so an early opportunity to introduce oneself by name helps to establish a personal place with other group members. This also allows the clients to choose the mode of address they prefer, whether it be the formal title (Mr, Ms, Mrs, Miss) and family name, first name or nickname. It also offers the opportunity for both therapist and group members to connect names to faces and remember them. To speak for the first time in a new group can be threatening, so the use of name games as an opening is invaluable in allaying some of the fears. Games which involve an object such as a ball or cushion deflect the focus of attention away from individuals. A popular game is for the group to stand (or sit) in a circle and to throw a ball to someone else saying their name loud enough for all to hear as they do. This can be extended to naming the person to whom the ball is being thrown, and still later by adding the name of the person to whom the recipient must then throw it. As the game becomes more complicated, it creates laughter and movement for a further release of anxiety. Alternatively, group members can be asked to introduce themselves to another member, who in turn introduces them to the group. Both methods allow the establishment of personality in a manner that eases tension.

### 'This is Daisy'

*It was the first day of the new group and a dozen anxious faces were spaced among the shadows at the edges of the room. Belinda, the dramatherapist looked round at everybody, smiling as she did so. 'I'm Belinda,' she reminded everybody.*

*'I've met you all at least once,' she said, 'but I guess there are things I don't know about you and you don't even know each other's names I think. Let's do something about that. In a moment, I'd like each of you to find a partner. When you have done that, spend a little time telling them about yourself – you'll have about five minutes each – I'll tell you when it is time to change. If you can, include something interesting or special about yourself, something we might not guess unless you told us – perhaps you have climbed Everest, perhaps you adore wearing pink socks. When you have done this, we'll get together again and each of you will have the chance to introduce the person you have been talking to – but don't worry – it isn't a memory test. Right, off you go.'*

*After a little nervous shuffling, everybody found a partner and the room soon filled with the buzz of animated conversation. Belinda told them when it was time to change and, after ten minutes, brought everybody together to sit in a circle next to their partner. 'Right,' said Belinda, 'Who wants to go first?' Shyly, Meeta and Daisy looked at each other and put up their hands. 'We will,' said Meeta. 'OK,' acknowledged Belinda, 'Off you go then.'*

*'This is Daisy,' said Meeta, 'She is 39 and has three kids – a boy and two girls (is that right Daisy?)'. Daisy nodded, smiling. 'Daisy won a beautiful baby competition when she was 8 months old but the most amazing thing about her is that she used to be a body builder!' Daisy, with a mock serious expression raised her arms in the traditional pose of a body builder showing of her biceps. The tension in the room dissolved in fits of affectionate, appreciative laughter.*

SPACE   The space where the group meets is very important. Ideally it should be created for the purpose of dramatherapy, but that is not always possible. There are however, certain minimum requirements. These are that the working area is:

- Private with no uncurtained windows that allow observation by others
- Free from the likelihood of interruption

- Warm but not hot
- Comfortable, but not so relaxing that people are reluctant to leave their chairs
- Furnished with enough upright chairs and/or cushions for all the group
- Free from any obstacles that may endanger or restrict movement
- Illuminated with lighting that is not too bright.

### *The women and the window cleaner*

*A group of women were exploring ways in which they could be assertive. They were working in pairs to produce a scenario to discuss with the group. The dramatherapist was surprised by a sudden silence in the room. There was a man at the window! As the room was on the second floor, it was most unexpected. No-one had thought to tell the therapist that the window cleaners were coming. There were no curtains to close and the women felt too conspicuous to continue with their action so sat down to talk. The therapist encouraged expression of their feelings of vulnerability at being observed and suggested that to continue with the session could be seen as asserting themselves. After much hesitant discussion, they finally agreed to leave their seats and resume their improvisation when the window cleaners were finishing the final window. It may have been a small compromise, but it was a big step for them requiring courage and self-confidence.*

CREATING BOUNDARIES  Therapy is often about learning that activities, people and systems have their limits. It is also reassuring for the client to know what the parameters of the dramatherapy group are – where fantasy ends and reality begins. The boundaries of dramatherapy include the physical, emotional and time limits. All these must be explicitly defined and held. In the case of physical boundaries, for example, this may be done by:

- Using a large piece of cloth or carpet on which all action takes place
- Outlining the space to be used with, for example, string, tape, ribbon, crepe paper

- Placing furniture to form a boundary
- Placing chairs in a circle inside which all action takes place
- If using a drama studio, ensuring that nothing belonging to another group or performance impinges on the therapy group space

These physical boundaries and the time limits of the session or a particular activity form a necessary framework for emotional boundaries.

### Peter's bark is worse than his bite

*The 'stage area' for the group was defined by a long piece of string laid across the floor. Peter was feeling very angry with his mother whom he thought was trying to run his life for him. Expressing his emotion allowed him to give vent to his violent feelings towards her. The therapist could see the potential danger in the situation, so she asked him what his anger looked like. He said it was like an angry dog straining at the leash, ready to maul his antagonist. Following this description, the therapist led him to the 'stage' and suggested he 'became' his anger. Taking on the role of the chained animal, he was able to feel the frustration that led to his anger. He asked for the lead to be removed, and immediately he felt less violent because he was not restrained. As he returned to the group, he felt he had left his anger behind in the stage area. Reflecting on the experience later, off stage, Peter was able to relate his frustration and some of his anger to the death three years earlier of his father for whom he had never grieved adequately. Following the sudden death of his father, he had been compliant towards his mother's wishes. He wanted to console his mother, denying his own feelings and trying to take his father's place. The metaphorical exploration of his anger helped him to understand its source and seek a new way of relating to his mother whilst paying attention to his own needs.*

### Robert gets some insight

*A group of young men were exploring ways of dealing with their anger. The space for action was marked by a circle of chairs. Robert was trying to confront his abusive father. Suddenly he shouted 'What's the use? He won't listen to me', and lunged forward at the man in role as his father. The dramatherapist intervened and removed him from the circle. Robert sat down and burst into tears. He talked about the anger he felt at home, and his father's inability to understand his frustration. He mentioned his brother who was in prison for aggravated burglary, and became aware of his father's anxiety that Robert should not follow the same route. When he returned to the scene with this insight, he was able to find another way to approach his father.*

Dramatherapy can arouse strong emotional responses and these too need to be boundaried in some way. For the most part, drama-therapists will work in such a way as to ensure that the session *per se* becomes a container for clients' emotional responses. It is not always possible to resolve everything in a single session but, at its close, group members can be asked to name anything from the session they would like to leave behind. These issues or feelings can then be metaphorically stored in a safe place till required, or discarded in a rubbish bin.

### Jack rescues righteous anger

*A group of adolescents with learning disabilities had been angry about a management decision to reduce their recre-ational space to allow for furniture storage whilst another room was redecorated. They worked with that anger in the dramatherapy session until they had reached an understand-ing of the temporary nature of the situation. At the end of the session they decided to dispose of all the angry feelings through the window. Each person imagined an object to represent their feelings and threw them out of the window. Sandra did not think that was complete and suggested washing them away by throwing a bucket of water after them. Jack hesitated, saying he may need his anger again. There was some discussion about completely disposing of the feelings because they realised that anger can sometimes be valuable if expressed in the right place and manner. Finally the dramatherapist suggested they find some way of saving sufficient righteous anger to use when necessary. Jack immediately produced an imaginary umbrella which he hung upside down from the window sill in order to catch some 'good anger'.*

## Forming working relationships

When used appropriately, the games, activities and techniques of dramatherapy become part of a therapeutic process. Healing lies within that process which is dependent on the relationship between therapist and clients together with the dramatic content. These combined generate the integration of coherence of thought, feeling and action. This can only happen in a trusting environment, so the first objective of dramatherapy is to facilitate a client's trust of the therapist and the other group members. This in part depends on a sense of containment and security, which are in turn dependent on reliable personal and group boundaries.

### Creating trust and group cohesion

Building trust is a primary objective of dramatherapy – without trust constructive change is unlikely. The dramatherapeutic medium offers trust building exercises of many kinds – but there is a paradox here. Trust exercises require trust! This includes trust in oneself, the dramatherapist and other group members. In order to create trust in others, therapists may be prepared to join in this part of the session. They also have a responsibility to observe the group in action and take care that no-one is hurt in the process.

It is essential that group members can trust each other and work to form an environment conducive to therapy. Games and exercises can be structured to encourage mutual trust and interdependence. For example both trust and co-operation are required when, working in pairs, sitting on the ground back to back, the pair link arms and try to get into an upright position – a physical task that not only promotes trust, but usually laughter and release of tension. It may be necessary to spend several sessions working with trust exercises and interactive games to promote an atmosphere in which personal work can take place. Unless the clients can really trust both the therapist and other group members there can be no sense of security.

Some examples of trust exercises are:

- The group stands up and forms a circle, each person stretching at arms length. In turns, each member leans as far forward as they can, the rest of the group adopting a stance to help them to balance and not fall.
- The group sits on the floor, holding hands, and together the group leans back as far as they can – to lying down if possible, then sit up together, still holding hands for support.

- The group forms a tight circle. One person goes into the centre, and with eyes closed allows him/herself to be passed from one person to another in the group.
- In pairs, one person leads another, who preferably has closed their eyes, around the room avoiding obstacles and being responsible for the welfare of their partner.
- In pairs, the couple experiment with different postures causing them to change the points of balance, for example, whilst holding on to each other's arms for support, they raise one leg from the ground, then swing it backwards and forwards. This can be repeated with the other leg.
- The group is divided into two parts. Each plans and creates an experience for the other, which entails the use of all the senses. Furniture, props and anything that creates sound, scent, tactile sensations and sight may be used. The first group then guides members of the second through the environment that they have created. The second group then invites the first group into the scene they have created. It is preferable that some of the senses be stimulated without sight (for example, something to be touched may be hidden in a bag or under a piece of material, something to be smelt may be in a container that does not allow it to be seen) but that will depend on the trust already in the group.

Many trust exercises require people to close their eyes. This can be very threatening for some clients, so care has to be taken to always offer the option of doing them with eyes open, or opening and closing eyes at will. Although dramatherapists may demonstrate activities that require eyes to be closed, they do not usually join in when the group is engaged in them, so that they can be watchful and ensure no-one and nothing comes to harm. However, by taking a leading role in balancing and supporting activities like those described above, dramatherapists can enter into the spirit of cohesive trust whilst still watching out for the security of others. Exercises that require one to be physically dependent on others encourages group cohesion and this leads to trust of a more personal nature, allowing exchange of personal information and sharing of feelings.

It is not always easy for people to have the confidence to perform trust exercises, but it is easy to promote a sense of 'dare' in some client groups. Care has to be taken that clients understand the purpose of the exercises and do not enter into a spirit of competition or daring.

### *Joan relaxes into trust*

*Joan was a very anxious person who initially found it diffi-
cult to trust other group members. She would cling tightly to
her neighbours when balancing and could not keep her eyes
closed for any length of time. She gradually learned to relax,
and one day she completed a 'blind' exercise without opening
her eyes. The group worked in pairs, one at each end of the
room. Partner A closed their eyes, while B directed them
through a maze of chairs to make contact. Joan was so
delighted with her achievement that she hugged her partner
Ruth saying 'I never thought I could trust anyone, but this
has proved that I can!'*

#### *Creating a sense of security*
Unless people feel comfortable and secure in the dramatherapy
group, they will not be able to achieve their goals. It is important
therefore to create a safe working environment for all dramatherapy
groups whatever client group or objectives. Most people feel anxious when they enter a new group of any description, and the
prospect of a therapy session can increase nervousness. It is not
possible or even advisable to allay all fears. A certain degree of tension encourages people to be alert, aware and interested in the
experience. Attention to some basic introductory components will
help to form a working relationship within the group. When boundaries have been established and the clients are aware of what is
acceptable, it is still important for them to have a sense of personal
security. Clients can feel very vulnerable during a dramatherapy
session but if they know beforehand that there is a 'safe place' for
them they are less likely to be anxious. There are a number of ways
in which safe places may be designated. Some suggestions are:

For each client to:

- Picture a place, either real or imagined in their mind's eye. Know
  that at any time they can picture that place and feel its sense of
  security.
- Find a space in the room that feels secure. At any time they can
  go to that place and feel its security.
- Create an imaginary place. Find their own space within that
  place and know that they can return in imagination at any time.

For the group (or the dramatherapist or both together) to:

- Build a 'den' in a corner of the room to which clients can return to feel its security.

### Jill takes the path to security

*A dramatherapy group had opted to create a scene on a desert island. As they were moving furniture to form boundaries, the dramatherapist asked if there was any way to leave the island. Jane suggested making a narrow pathway that was accessible at low tide. As the improvisation progressed, Jill became anxious and tearful. She found the path, left the island and sat watching the group for a while. When she regained her composure she returned to the improvisation. At the close of the session she shared her experience with the group. In her role in the scene she had been the victim of an angry mob. It had reminded her of a time when she had been at a football match and the crowd had become aggressive. She was so upset by the memory that she had to leave the scene and role. As she watched the improvisation, she saw how others were coping with the state of affairs, and was even able to laugh at the behaviour of someone who was taking a clown role. On returning to the scene, she was able to cope with the situation, by behaving in role very differently than she had previously. Jill felt that by retreating to a safe place and observing others, she had gained a new way of responding to violence which she could transfer to reality.*

### Structure
A further major choice to be made is the structure of the session. This may be one of three main forms of dramatherapy and it is important to select the one most appropriate for the client(s) and the issues to be explored. The dramatherapy sessions may be:

- Completely unplanned and spontaneous
- Loosely structured with a wide scope for spontaneous development
- Tightly structured allowing for spontaneity only within the given framework.

Although spontaneity is basic to dramatherapy, sessions cannot take place in a vacuum. It is essential that the dramatherapist has an overall plan of action. Indeed, there is a conventional, tried and tested shape to a dramatherapy session regardless of which of the three above styles is adopted. Dramatherapy sessions are usually structured to contain three phases:

1   Warm-up in which the group re-establishes itself and prepares for action (for example a name game, trust exercise as mentioned above, or a very active game such as 'tag')
2   A period of focused activity which may consist of any dramatic experience (for example, taking on fantasy roles in an improvisation)
3   Closure – a time for reflection and preparation to return to reality (for example, a ritual allowing group members to disengage from roles they may have played and the features that go with them and to pick up any attributes they may have laid aside for the duration of the session).

Unplanned and spontaneous sessions   In an unplanned session, when, the clients enter the dramatherapy space, they are free to play with any props or just to move around alone or mingle and interact with each other until a theme arises or a scene is enacted spontaneously. Dramatherapists act as facilitator and guide, following the clients' ideas and possibly contributing to the action themselves.

### Returning to school

*A group of people resident in an addiction unit entered the dramatherapy space directly after a tense community meeting. Hannah picked up a ball and threw it to Joan, who bounced it around the room, until Hannah gave chase and wrested the ball from her. Other group members joined in and soon the group had formed two sides, playing 'pass the ball'. A great deal of energy was expended until someone said 'It's like a school playground'. The group then spontaneously transformed the room, marking the netball pitch, the classrooms and the school gate. They proceeded to behave like children at playtime, some playing ball, others skipping and racing with each other. Joan began to tease Hannah saying 'You can't catch me – you're too fat'. A brawl ensued in which others joined. Martha, another group member, took on the role of teacher and calmed the situation, telling them all that they would have to stay indoors at lunch break and write 'I must not fight' a hundred times. At this point, Hannah started to cry, but still in role said she had to go home to see her mother who was ill. The group then moved to the scene at lunch time, where Hannah left the class to go home, knowing she was in further trouble. She separated herself from the group and watched while they played out the classroom scene. At the end of the session, the group de-roled and shared the experience. Hannah was again tearful, and recounted an episode when she was pregnant as a teenager. Afraid to tell anyone, she had been taunted by friends because she was putting on weight. She was comforted by group members and made a contract to do further personal work on the issue. All the group members agreed that the regression into childhood had allowed them to 'let off steam' after the earlier tense group meeting. They then likened their current situation in the unit with its strict regime to school experiences, and the need for external help, which felt like control, in their efforts to overcome their addictive behaviour. The session had operated on both a personal and a group level.*

LOOSELY STRUCTURED SESSIONS WITH A WIDE SCOPE FOR SPONTANEOUS DEVELOPMENT   This format can be pre-planned by the therapist if a particular issue has previously arisen. Alternatively, as the session commences, the group can re-establish itself by individuals discussing their activities since they last met and naming any feelings or matters that are important at the moment and thus decide on a topic for exploration. The therapist may suggest a structure, listening to their ideas and incorporating them as the session progresses. Or the group may decide the topic and structure for themselves.

### The students work with time and space

*A group of students in a therapy group shared their experiences of the past week. There were two issues that arose in the discussion and they found it difficult to select one for further exploration. The therapist suggested that the group divided into two, each section working on its own issue. One sub-group, which felt under pressure at work and at college, selected the theme of time. The therapist suggested they started by creating a clock. At first they physically formed a clock face and became numerals, hands, chimes and alarm. Each person made a statement from their position that expressed their feelings. The hands said that they could not move fast enough, the numerals complained of being inactive, the chimes felt they were not heard, and the alarm felt she possessed the dominant role in the clock. After discussing the implication of the sculpt (as it is termed), each person found a space of their own, and continued their exploration by creating a sequence of movements, which they later performed to the rest of their small group.*

*There had been a sense of unease the previous session when the group met in a different studio because their usual space was required for examinations. The second group still felt disturbed by this event and decided to explore the space. They spontaneously moved around their section of the room, at first avoiding all physical contact, gradually acknowledging each other by touch, eye contact or speech until they gathered to share current feelings, which were around being crowded and usurped. They decided to improvise a situation where a group of squatters were being 'moved on'. Jan took on the role of the underdog who constantly complained about the situation but felt powerless to do anything. Rod became the political planner, who came into conflict with Pete who was trying to negotiate with the evictors. Polly and Mike took on the roles of the policewoman and housing manager. The squatters tried initially to 'sit it out', but after some physical intervention from the evictors, they eventually had to leave. They then repeated the scene, but this time Rod took on the role of mediator. In the ensuing discussion, they realised that the mediation was more effective than defiance and related that to their current situation. They decided to appeal to the course tutor for better facilities and more time for relaxation as a group.*

*When the whole group came together at the close of the session, they realised that in fact, both groups had been working on the same topic – that of personal space and time for oneself.*

TIGHTLY STRUCTURED SESSIONS   Tightly structured sessions offer the dramatherapist a degree of control (and the clients the safety inherent in that control) which is desirable or even necessary on some occasions or with certain client groups. There are three reasons to create a tightly structured session. These are when:

1   The client group is unable to structure for themselves, for example, people with dementia or severe learning disabilities
2   There is a need for some form of restraint, for example, when working with people with behavioural difficulties
3   The clients are to work on a specific issue.

### *From tag to negotiation*

*There was tension amongst a group of young men in a forensic unit who became rebellious when there was an alteration in their working timetable which left less time for television viewing hours. They arrived at the dramatherapy group expressing anger and displeasure, grumbling that the staff treated them like children. Their immediate reaction was to confront the ward staff in an aggressive manner. The dramatherapist, having been previously appraised of the situation, devised a session to look at other means of approach.*

*The warm-up was an energetic game of tag. One person was 'it'. When he touched another person, that person stood still with legs astride, and could then be 'released' for further play if another group member crawled under his legs. The physical activity helped to dispel some of the angry energy with which they had entered the room. The next step was still physical, but less energetic. The group stood in a circle, facing inwards. One person, Alan, had a bean bag and ran round the outside of the circle and dropped it behind Brian who chased him. Whoever reached the space in the group first would join the group; the other would take the bean bag and repeat the procedure. A second bean bag was introduced and then a third, so that there were three chases happening simultaneously.*

*The next step was a tug-of-war in pairs. The group was paired according approximately to height and weight, a line*

*was drawn across the centre of the room and each tried to
pull the other across the line.*

*The group then sat down and shared their feelings of the
session so far. John admitted that he had felt he would like to
fight with the nursing staff at the beginning of the session.
Douglas said that he would have liked a tug-of-war with the
staff nurse, because he could have won. Mike admitted that
his feelings were less violent having used up some energy.
Others agreed that they were feeling less angry, but still dis-
contented with affairs.*

*The dramatherapist then suggested a negotiating game. John
left the room and devised an action he wanted them to perform – to move a table from one side of the room to the other.
The other group members decided upon an action they wanted
him to perform – to open a particular window. On his return,
John negotiated movements with the group. He asked Douglas
and Mike to move six steps towards the table. They agreed to
do it if John walked six steps to the left. Each negotiation took
the protagonist nearer the goal set for him, until eventually
John reached the window, but before he was asked to open it,
the table was shifted into position. The group enjoyed the
sense of competition and repeated the exercise several times
with different members.*

*Following some discussion of the game, the therapist then
divided the group into pairs to discuss means of negotiation
with the ward staff about the new rules, and what they, as a
group, could offer in exchange for revision of the new scheme.
This was followed by role play, in which individual members
demonstrated how they would approach the ward staff.*

Once the nature of the dramatherapy contract is accepted and
the clients and dramatherapist have begun to know each other and
established some trust in the group, then the ground is prepared for
dramatherapy sessions proper.

# 4

# BEGINNING A DRAMATHERAPY SESSION

Normally, a dramatherapy group will take a particular form. It will begin with a warm-up, simple or elaborate depending on the needs of the group and the intended focus of the session. Then comes an action phase that constitutes the substance of the session, which may take various forms and use one or more of a number of techniques. Finally, when the drama is completed, there will be an end phase offering a chance to de-role and for closure. The duration of these phases will vary. Perhaps a new group will spend longer warming up than a mature group. Maybe a particularly intense action will require longer for de-roling, emotional processing and closure. As a general rule, the form is always the same. This is equally true when a dramatherapy session has a particular emphasis (for example, social skills training or reminiscence therapy) although in this case the warm-up is likely to focus on the same area as the forthcoming action phase.

## *Warming-up*

Dramatherapy sessions will normally start with an opportunity for the group members including the dramatherapist to warm-up, that is, to become focused on the session and to be mentally and physically prepared for dramatherapeutic action. Warm-ups come in many shapes and sizes and are multifunctional. Cattanach (1994a: 37) describes the warm-up as preparation time which 'sets the mood, themes and focus for the rest of the session'. It also introduces the tools of drama. Jones (1996: 19) points out that the dramatherapy warm-up can address one or more of several key areas. These are:

- Body/mind – including physical co-ordination, concentration and physical expression
- Working with others – for example, engaging in physical activity with others and working with emotions with others
- Use of materials – such as using objects physically, using them imaginatively and projecting feeling into material
- Issues – including group or individual topics.

Warm-ups can be as simple as passing a baton to each person in turn who then states how they are feeling at the moment (for example). Or they can be energetic games to literally warm-up physically. Perhaps because of their association with play and childhood, games of 'tag' and chase are popular with many groups.

### Chasing away cares

*A hospital staff training group met weekly immediately after work for a dramatherapy training session. Initially the group members asked to do something energetic because the room was cold. The game of 'tag' that ensued was boisterous, lively and well received. As the room was always cold at the end of the day energetic children's games became a ritual beginning. The participants felt that the sense of play helped them to discard the thoughts and feelings of the working day and helped them to re-orientate themselves by concentrating on the moment, leaving minds clear for the action stage.*

So, dramatherapy warm-ups may offer group members an opportunity to:

1 Get to know each other and to introduce themselves to the group
2 Prepare their bodies for what at times may be a fairly robust activity
3 Focus on their physical being
4 Awaken imagination and creative potential.

The warm-up is also an opportunity for the dramatherapist to introduce the elements of drama which may be used in that particular session and also those that might be used in subsequent ones.

## Introductory warm-ups

Introductory warm-ups are intended to be 'ice-breakers', giving opportunities for forming relationships and establishing one's place in the group. Each dramatherapy session will normally begin with one or more warm-up exercises. This is in order to release any tensions group members may have and turn their attention to the therapeutic milieu. There is a direct parallel with warming-up to physical activity but in the case of a dramatherapy warm-up mind and spirit are being focused on and prepared as well as body. Also, the warm-up is not just of the individuals but between them (warming-up to being part of the group) and to the working space. Different groups have different attitudes to warming-up. Some enjoy the novelty of a new approach each time, while other groups find safety and reassurance in familiarity repeatedly requesting a particular activity, so creating a ritual beginning to the session. Ritual can contribute to a sense of group identity and purpose.

### The beanbag beginning

*A group of people with long-term mental health problems enjoyed throwing a beanbag round the circle and calling their name. It was initially a method of establishing identity, but it became an important opening for them. Even when they had been together as a group for ten weeks, they still asked to 'play the name game' which took on the ritual function of providing a sense of security.*

Warm-ups can also be introductory in that they prepare for the theme of the session. A tug-of-war either in teams or in pairs, for example, can warm people physically as well as set the atmosphere for a theme of conflict. Before embarking on the issues for the session, it is important to prepare the group or individual. A warm-up aimed at awakening and energising the group and which allows them to 'step into' the session, should precede one introducing a particular theme. Warm-ups are intended to prepare clients for action. They may be part of a planned structure (that is, the dramatherapist may have a theme in mind and have chosen one or more appropriate exercises to warm-up to it), or spontaneously evolve into another dramatic activity – for example, playing with a football may recall bullying at school and lead to an improvisation on the subject of intimidation. The dramatherapist will be aware of the potential and if it is appropriate will follow the group's lead and encourage further development.

## Physical warm-ups

Sometimes it is appropriate or important to offer a dramatherapy group the opportunity to warm-up physically. This may be in a quite literal sense but it is also about raising energy levels and preparing to be physically active in the main portion of the session. Physical warm-ups also allow group members to relax their minds, freeing them from unwanted thoughts and feelings. A physical warm-up exercise may be followed by a sequence of games and/or exercises that expand the theme. Examples of physical warm-ups include those based on childhood games, those using equipment of some kind and those designed to create some kind of action.

### Warm-ups based on childhood games

- Games of tag – any number of variations on simple chase games where one person is 'it' and chases others until some contact is made. The touched person then becomes 'it' and thus the pursuer, and so on.
- Grandma's footsteps – one person is selected as 'grandma' and stands with their back to the rest of the group who try to creep forward, their objective being to make it to the finishing line without being caught in motion by 'grandma', who, at any time may turn round and try to catch anyone who is moving. Any person caught then returns to the start line and recommences their efforts.
- Off-ground touch – a variation on tag where the person who is 'it' tries to catch other group members. The pursued can become immune if they stand on a chair or step or any other designated raised object.

- Musical chairs/bumps – group members walk around the room to music. When the music stops they must try to find a chair and sit on it. If they do not, they are 'out'. Chairs are gradually withdrawn to reduce the competition – the last person left is the winner. A similar game can be played by sitting on the floor (bumps) – when the music stops the last person to sit down is 'out'.
- What's the time Mr. Wolf? – one person stands with their back to the rest of the group who try to creep up to them. The group chants 'What's the time Mr. Wolf?' at intervals. The wolf calls a variety of times remaining with his back to them. When he says 'Dinner time' they all run away and he tries to catch them. ·
- Follow the leader – one person walks around the room and everyone follows, copying the leader's actions.

### Warm-up games using equipment

Games can be simply active passing of objects, or competitive games. It is important to be aware of competition and only encourage it if it is appropriate to the group and the theme. For example, if the group is trying to encourage self-assertion, then competition is relevant, but if the theme is concerned with co-operation then it is not. Any equipment should be used with care and forethought. Some clients may be afraid of being hurt, others may want to take advantage of physical prowess and behave in a dangerous manner. A blow on the head from a hard ball is potentially dangerous. Elderly or physically disadvantaged clients may be unsteady on their feet and apt to fall if the game becomes too vigorous. Bearing all this in mind, some of the games employing equipment from which a dramatherapist may choose include:

- Passing a ball or beanbag round a circle (this can be combined with a name game, see above)
- In teams, spinning a hoop, in turns each person tries to catch it before it falls to the ground
- Team games of passing a ball or beanbag
- In pairs, throwing and catching a ball using only one hand
- Throwing a ball/beanbag round the circle, anyone who fails to catch it has a penalty such as using only one hand or standing on one leg etc.
- Sitting in two rows, facing each other, group members pat a balloon to each other, trying not to leave their seats
- In teams, standing, pass the ball to each other trying to keep it off the ground.

### Simple warm-up activities to create action

As well as games from childhood and those using simple equipment such as balls, beanbags or hoops, dramatherapists have other physical activities available to them as warm-ups. These include:

- Running and touching a particular object or set of objects (for example, a window, door, chair and curtain) before returning to their places. A variation is to locate objects with particular qualities, for example, something red, something blue, something yellow and then returning
- Following one of them designated as the leader, running around the room touching (say) four objects and returning to their starting points
- Joining hands in a line, the leader taking the rest of the group around the room walking in a specific rhythm. The group follows and each member in turn changes the rhythm of the movement.

## Mental and imaginative warm-ups

The objectives of warm-ups focusing on activities of the mind rather than the body include:

- Preparing group members for intellectual activity such as decision-making
- Stimulating thought in order to engender creativity
- Creating a focus on the topic to be explored.

As with physical warm-ups, dramatherapists have a pool of activities upon which they can draw and they use their experience and professional judgement to decide which activities are appropriate for a particular group, time and place. Some suitable activities are:

1  The group members sit in a circle. An object such as a piece of cloth or scarf is passed around them. Each person creates something from it and tells and/or shows the rest of the group what it has become in their imagination – for example, it can be a hat, a table cloth, a lion's tail or an elephant's trunk.
2  Each group member is invited to think of a flower. The first person names their's, the next one repeats this and names

their own, the third repeats the flowers already named and adds another, and so on until the last person has a long list to remember.

3   Each person makes a statement about the topic for the day – for example, if the focus is to be on the senses, everyone can be invited to name a particular smell or sight they would like to experience again.

## Emotional warm-ups

As the heading suggests, there are warm-up techniques that are designed to put participants in touch with their feelings and to encourage a focus on one particular emotional response. These warm-ups may also increase the emotional repertoire of participants. Emotional warm-ups may also be geared towards discovering what emotions are connected with particular events or memories. Useful activities include inviting group members to:

- Write an imaginary letter to someone who has angered them in order to encourage introspection and explore feelings around a topic.
- Think of someone whom they have not seen for a long time. What would they like to say to them?
- Become a character in a book or play and think about that character's history, the part it plays in the story and the way it relates to other people. How much of their own personality do they see in the character?
- Use other members of the group to create a picture. It could be an imitation of a real picture, painting or photograph. Or it could be an entirely imaginary one. The person who created it is then asked if there is anyone in the picture who reminds them of someone they know? If so, what would they like to say to them?
- Imagine lying under a tree on a hot summer day. Who would they like to join them and why?
- Think of a character in a play or book who they would like to play. What is appealing about that character?

Sometimes imaginative warm-ups lead directly to more personal work. For example:

### Enchanting Jo

*A dramatherapy group had been exploring the story of Shakespeare's play* The Tempest, *and improvising around some of the scenes. The next session, the dramatherapist asked the group to think about the play and concentrate on one particular character. Jo found the wizardry of Prospero intriguing, and wanted to cast magic spells. When asked to explore the reason for this, she said that she would like to cast a spell on her parents as they did not understand her. This highlighted for her the possibility of altering her way of relating to them. At a later session, Jo was able to look at the relationship psychodramatically and find a new understanding of her parents.*

In this example, Jo was 'warmed-up' to her relationship with her parents. With the help of the dramatherapist (who was also a trained psychodramatist), and the agreement of the rest of the group, she went on to explore this relationship in a particular way, that is, through the medium of psychodrama. Psychodrama is an action method of psychotherapy related to dramatherapy in that it makes use of action and role (see Wilkins, 1999).

Although emotional warm-ups are usually intended to create material for work in the session, sometimes immediate work is inappropriate. For example, if there is not sufficient time to look in depth at an issue, it can be discussed and agreed to be a subject for the next session. It is always important to work at the client's own pace, and it may be necessary to postpone work until the client feels ready. Any attempt to force people to explore issues unwillingly is not only counter-therapeutic but also unethical.

# 5

# APPLYING
# DRAMATHERAPY

In dramatherapy, warm-up is a prelude to 'action' but action comes in many shapes and sizes. It may comprise one or more structured exercises each with a specific objective. It may be the making and telling of a story or an improvised piece of a theatrical play, the theme of which emerged from the warm-up. Or it may be any one of a number of things. What follows is an account of some of the applied functions of an action phase of dramatherapy and examples appropriate to particular aims.

## *Interaction*

Like other group approaches to psychotherapy, dramatherapy depends upon group cohesion and at least basic levels of group trust for its efficiency and accomplishment. Without these, the interaction necessary for successful implementation of the structures and techniques of dramatherapy cannot happen. It follows that amongst the first tasks of the dramatherapist is to promote and facilitate interaction between group members. For example, when a group of people meet who do not know each other well, or have not met for a short time, some form of introduction or 'ice-breaking' is needed. There is also a need to focus on the session and the task in hand. Some ways in which dramatherapists may help group members in 'meeting' each other are for each participant to:

- Walk around the room concentrating on their own movement and style and ignoring other people. To then gradually become aware of others but not to interact with them. Next to greet other group members they meet but to do so non-verbally. The next stage is for each group member to speak to others as they pass. This exercise may continue for as long as it takes for everyone to encounter every other group member at least once. It may be curtailed at any time the dramatherapist thinks its objectives have been achieved.
- Find a partner and to tell them about the journey to the session. Alternatively, if the notion of journeying to the dramatherapy session is not appropriate, the story may be of some other daily activity, for example, the daily ritual of getting up in the morning.
- Greet everyone else in the room in a different manner. For example, this may involve physical acts or gestures – a bow or a wave, differences in tone or volume (a shy whisper, a glad shout) or any other safe, non-threatening action the dramatherapist or individual group member may suggest.
- In pairs, take turns in describing to their partners a familiar place perhaps with which they have pleasant associations and/or feelings of safety or comfort. Each group member then takes an imaginary walk into their partners' environment, closing eyes (if possible) and concentrating on the textures, scents and sounds they would experience if they were really there.
- Find a partner they do not know very well and to tell them their life story. However, the life story is told with a mixture of truth and lies. Can the partner guess the lies?

## *Group cohesion*

Group cohesion grows through interaction and exercises which promote contact and engender an initial level of trust. It is only as a group begins to develop a sense of identity, of 'us', that the real work of dramatherapy can begin. Therefore, it is sometimes useful to extend the exercises aimed at facilitating group interaction into those which focus more on group cohesion until it is appropriate to embark on dramatherapy itself. These may be useful team-building exercises or may lead in to further improvisation. Some examples include:

1   The group becomes a ship-building team. Using the furniture and apparatus in the room, they are to build a boat in which they can move. The group collectively plans the way in which they will work. From within the group, roles are allocated – manager, foremen, skilled worker, labourer etc. Together, in accordance with their designated roles, the group members carry out the plan.

2   The group members take on the roles of shipwrecked sailors. Together they build shelter, care for each other, forage for food and plan a means of returning home.

3   The group becomes an orchestra with no appointed leader. One person selects the first instrument. Then they all enact playing the same instrument. Without recourse to a designated leader and with no discussion, each person in turn changes the instrument. This exercise requires that attention be paid to everyone in the group and it is only by co-operation that the sequence can be co-ordinated.

4   The group form a line holding hands, the first person in the line becoming its leader. The leader then takes the line round the room avoiding obstacles. Next, the leader interweaves with the others by going underneath their arms to form a human knot. The group members then decide how to disentangle themselves without breaking the linkage of hands.

### Nursing team spirit

*A group of student nurses were disturbed by administrative changes which strengthened the staff hierarchical system. They asked to explore the issue in a dramatherapy group. The dramatherapist asked for suggestions on a theme of team work and they decided to build a boat. In the first improvised construction, the group formed a strict hierarchy of workers who gave and received orders according to their status. The boat was speedily and easily constructed using furniture and props in the drama studio. The dramatherapist then suggested they create another boat, but this time each person worked as a individual, contributing as they felt necessary. The result was chaotic, with people undoing work others had constructed, fighting over materials, and spending time in discussing conflicting ideas. At the end of the session the group were able to look at the staffing issue with a different perspective and consider their own roles within the nursing hierarchy.*

Although exercises to promote interaction and group cohesion have their primary function in the early stage of the work of a dramatherapy group, it may be necessary and/or desirable to return to them at a later time. For example, if there is dissention in the group, then an exercise involving co-operation and collaboration may serve as a reminder to the group of the usefulness of working together. In this way clients are reminded that they are not working in isolation but have formed a working relationship and a group identity. Where it is appropriate and likely to be helpful, it is possible to move to specific issues such as social or negotiation skills and to address these dramatherapeutically.

## Negotiation

Good negotiating skills are an essential part of social being. Just as children learn negotiation through play (see Cattanach, 1994a: 31; 1994b: 140) and this is a useful lesson for life, so, through dramatic play, dramatherapy may supply similar learning. Both can be an aid to the function and purpose of the dramatherapy group and a model for its members to apply more widely in other spheres of their lives. Cattanach (1994b: 140) points out that negotiation involves the acceptance of someone's ideas and the rejection of others. A vital lesson on how to deal with direction can be learned from this. Negotiation can also involve lessons in compromise and reaching an effective consensus. In the negotiating dramatherapy group, the emotional and cognitive mechanisms of each individual interact with their innate creativity. In turn this interacts with the dynamics of the group. It is from the interplay of these forces that the creative potential of the group as a whole emerges. Some examples of how an experience of negotiation may be offered to a dramatherapy group are:

1   In pairs, one person takes on the role of home occupier while the other becomes a potential buyer who is shown around the house. The occupant does not really want to sell; the buyer is keen to buy. The partners interact together in their designated roles with the potential buyer trying to persuade the seller to

part with the property while the occupier resists and attempts to dissuade the buyer.

2   The group is divided into two. One half takes the role of a family on a seaside picnic, the second becomes a party of students celebrating their examination results in a rowdy manner. The two parties meet on the beach and a meeting is improvised.

3   In pairs, one person is a gardener who has lit a bonfire in his garden, the other is a neighbour who complains about the smoke and dust reaching his own garden. In an improvised action, the two partners each express their points of view.

The usefulness of the exercises in negotiation lies in both the actual experience and in reflecting on it. It is usual to have a long period of discussion at the end of the session during which individuals can express new ideas on the matter, and to practise some of these new ways of negotiating, or commit the next session to developing dramatisation of some new negotiating skills.

## Social skills training

In some settings, the action phase of dramatherapy may be less concerned with facilitating some positive change to the emotional and mental being of the participants and more to do with behaviour or the acquisition of skills. For example, clients who have been receiving psychiatric treatment for a long time, people in residential care and those who have never related successfully to others may benefit from training in social skills. Drama encompasses a number of attributes required for socialisation and so is an excellent medium for training. A course in social skills may start at a basic level, such as learning to make eye contact with the person with whom you are conversing. Depending on the needs and abilities of their members, groups may begin social skills training at different levels leading to effective verbal communication and progress through to role play of difficult situations. Whatever the level of practice, games are a means of learning in action which is the essence of dramatherapy. Examples of useful games with a social skills function are:

*   With the group standing in a circle, one person is asked to signal the intent to change places with another by winking at them. In response to the wink, the second person changes place with the

first and then takes on the 'wink' message, changing places with another group member and so on.

- Standing in a circle, group members each find a partner by using eye contact only. The conversation of the partners centres on paying and receiving compliments. Each partner makes a personal comment to the other, for example, one may say 'I like your dress' and the other finds a suitable reply – 'Thank you, I like the way you've had your hair cut'. The conversation continues for as long as seems appropriate. The exercise may be expanded by everybody finding another partner and making and receiving more compliments.
- In pairs, group members take on roles of two people sitting on a park bench. One has come for a quiet time away from a noisy office. The other is a lonely person who is looking for company. How does each of them cope with their individual needs?

As a way of processing and consolidating the learning from the above, and similar exercises, group members may discuss them first in pairs and then in the group as a whole. They may, for example, consider the part that eye contact, observation of others and careful listening play in the art of conversation.

## Exercises to promote awareness of surroundings

There are some people for whom making and maintaining successful social contact is problematic as a result of long periods of limited interpersonal relationships such as being in hospital or a residential home. There are others for whom simply connecting with the world is difficult, perhaps as the result of impairment present from birth, brought about by accident, infirmity or the ageing process. Dramatherapy, with its underpinning of learning through play and dramatic action is an ideal way of enhancing the connection a person has with their surroundings.

There are a number of simple dramatherapeutic activities which promote an awareness of surroundings and/or use senses of touch, smell and sight to enhance day-to-day living. Reality orientation helps with that awareness while reminiscence therapy aids memory and also assists clients to come to terms with ageing, past life and the present. Physical exercise helps to keep joints active. All address the difficulties of elderly, long-stay clients in residential or day care units, people experiencing memory problems or severe learning disabilities and people who are likely to be disorientated or take their environment for granted. The following exercises are appropriate in such settings but, because dramatherapy is versatile and works on many levels, they can also be used as a warm-up with any group. They can also be used for other purposes, for example, to promote a sense of alertness and familiarity with the work place.

- Group members are encouraged to walk around the room touching the walls, furniture and any objects they encounter. They are encouraged to experience a wide range of textures and to reflect on what they feel. What feels the nicest? What the most unpleasant? After the active part of the exercise, each person shares their experience with a partner.
- Walking around the room, each person makes sounds by tapping, scraping or banging on the objects they encounter. Selecting the object of which they most like the sound, everyone beats out a rhythm. Each group member then joins with two other people to create a rhythmical composition.
- The group members study the angles and shapes in the room. Then, in twos or threes, group members try to recreate them with their bodies.
- Group members may be asked to number and name the colours they can see in the room and perhaps to name a favourite.

Each of the above exercises involves the group members in encountering some aspect or aspects of their environment. This can have real benefits on the sense of self and general well-being.

### Lily's curtains

*A group of clients who had been hospitalised for a long time were members of a dramatherapy group. As a warm-up, the dramatherapist asked them to touch something red, something blue and something green and return to their places. Lily, walking with the aid of a zimmer frame was the last to arrive back to her chair. On her return, she was pleased that she had walked so far and also said: 'I've been in this ward for three years, and I never knew the curtains were so pretty, they have lovely red and pink roses on them'.*

By encouraging her to be active, in however small a way, the dramatherapist helped Lily to expand her view of the world. Lily awoke from the passive state into which she had slipped, enjoyed finding that she was not as physically limited as she had come to believe and found that even in the narrow confines of her ward there were things to be experienced and enjoyed. This, and her subsequent experiences with the dramatherapy group, enriched Lily's daily life.

## Exercises emphasising the senses

We pay varying amounts of attention to our awareness of the information emanating from our five senses. Concentrating more directly on one or more of the senses and what it tells about the surroundings can be valuable in a number of ways. In dramatherapy, becoming focused on sensory input is a way of grounding group members, bringing them to the 'here and now'. It is also about broadening and sharpening awareness which may be useful for anybody but which has particular value when working with people who tend to be out of touch with their immediate surroundings and the people around them. Also games and exercises involving seeing, smelling, hearing, tasting and touching can be fun – and fun has a function promoting cohesion. Examples of dramatherapy exercises that encourage participants to focus on the senses include:

- The dramatherapist asks clients to close their eyes and become aware of all the sounds there are in the room and to identify them. Group members are then encouraged to listen to all the sounds they can hear that are outside the room, but in the building. The focus of listening then extends to the sounds that are outside the building. Amongst other things, this exercise has the effect of expanding the zone of awareness of the participants.
- The dramatherapist supplies a bag containing a variety of objects that are interesting to touch (for example, a piece of satin or silk, a pouch of beans, some sand paper, nuts and bolts etc.). The group sit in a circle and pass the bag around. Each person puts a hand into the bag and tries to identify an object and comment on how it feels to them.
- The dramatherapist supplies a variety of pots containing different scents. The group try to identify the contents by their smell. Smell is probably the most evocative of senses and during this exercise

group members are often stimulated to remember ·particular associations they have with particular smells. If it is appropriate and there is sufficient time, the telling of the individual stories provoked by the smells can become a further enriching aspect to this exercise.

- In pairs, the client studies their partner's clothes. Each person turns away and alters something of their clothing. The partner observes what has changed. Besides emphasising sight, this exercise encourages interaction and contact between group members.
- The dramatherapist invites clients to think of a place that is familiar to them, then asks the group to try to remember all the colours in it and, using paper and art materials supplied by the dramatherapist, to paint a 'rainbow' using all those colours.
- The dramatherapist shows the group a picture and asks them what they see. Group members may then be encouraged to explore what they like and dislike about the picture.

Dramatherapy functions in more than one way. The above exercises demonstrate this. They all focus on sensory perception with the effects indicated above, but do something else as well. For example, some encourage interaction and/or self-expression; others foster memory and in any or all there may be playfulness and fun with all the benefits thereof.

## Dramatherapy with older people

Dramatherapy has an important part to play in all aspects of work with the elderly, including doing reality orientation and reminiscence therapy (see below). Langley and Langley (1983: 39–53) have written widely on the subject, suggesting various suitable dramatic activities. Lahad (see Jennings, 1994: 181–2), stresses the 'great need' for dramatherapists to work with the elderly people and stated that, in his experience, 'a group with the elderly is always successful'. Mitchell (1994: 42–4) has written of his use of dramatherapy with elderly people and demonstrates the effectiveness of his work.

### Reality orientation
Clients whose memory is poor, or who become confused as a result of their illness, are usually introduced to a process of 'reality orientation' in which they are frequently reminded of time and place to assist them to stay within the bounds of reality. In both

day care and residential settings for people with these characteristics (frequently the elderly), there is usually a noticeboard displaying information to help promote contact with the 'here and now' and to gently remind clients when and where they are – for example, time, date and current affairs. Staff take every opportunity to clarify the environment for their clients and dramatherapists working with them combine reminders of reality in their sessions. Ways in which this may be done include encouraging participants to:

- Look at the orientation board and to notice what is new that day
- Look around the room and tell a partner how to get to a particular place – perhaps the toilet or (in residential settings) the bedroom
- Look out of the window and notice what can be seen. For example, what plants are there? Are there leaves on the trees? What time of the year is it?
- Look at the clothes people outside are wearing. What do they tell about the weather forecast?
- Look at the dining area and decide from what can be seen what the next meal will be
- The dramatherapist brings seasonal fruits such as blackberries or flowers like daffodils into the group and asks what they tell about the season.

Exercises designed to promote reality orientation are of necessity simple but they may nevertheless be relatively taxing for the participants and far-reaching in their effects:

### Mabel's squirrel

*There was a row of beautiful chestnut trees in full flower outside the building in which a group of clients suffering from dementia met for the dramatherapy group. The group were taken to the window and asked what they could see and what the scene told them about the time of year. As they were admiring the trees, Mabel saw a squirrel run across a branch. She was reminded of her childhood and the fact she used to feed the squirrels in the autumn. Although she was usually confused, the memory helped her, for a brief period to clearly define the difference in scenery from spring to autumn, which stimulated some response from other group members.*

## Reminiscence

The object of reminiscence therapy is to promote life review. Langley (Langley and Langley, 1983: 142) has written on this and states that amongst other things, it aids 'the updating of values and lifestyle in which the present is met by drawing from a lifetime of experiences'. It can also serve as a means of preserving local history and keeping traditions alive. The days when old people were valued as storytellers seemed to have passed, but recently oral history has started to take its place among the archives. Tape recorded interviews, photograph albums, storytelling and written memories can become a focus of interest in a group. It may be possible to find a wider audience by visits to or from school children, writing in church and village news-letters, and possibly brief presentations of scripted or improvised theatre. Elderly people are sometimes considered boring when they frequently recount the same life events, but it is important to remember the human need to 'gain a perspective' and validate one's life and achievements. These are important at any age, but particularly in the elderly. Helping to keep memories alive assists this process, and often stimulates interaction as people share recollections and exchange ideas. It also shows appreciation of the contribution that people have made during their life time, aids self-esteem and values them as individuals. Reminiscence therapy can take different forms such as:

- Storytelling around a theme (schooldays, war-time experiences, coronations, the advent of television).
- Use of scripts and improvisations. A group of staff or group members read a scene from a play that the group members are likely to know (for example, a script by Noel Coward). This can provoke memories and discussion of a particular period or event.
- Ballroom dancing (or other forms of dancing that participants did in their youth) for the physically active.
- Creation of photographic records – participants may be willing to donate or loan 'snaps' from their personal albums but copies of archive material from, for example, the local press or muse-ums may be useful in building up a collection to illustrate an historical aspect of, say, the immediate locality. Postcard albums may be similarly compiled and it may be possible to arrange slide presentations of historical material.
- Drawings and paintings by group members or borrowed from collections.

- Display of the tools, kitchen implements, clothing and hats of yesteryear as focus for discussion.
- Purposely created theatre around group members' memories. This requires involvement of a theatre group who are prepared to research and produce an entertainment (see Langley and Langley, 1983: 146).
- Music is an immediate means of evoking memories and it also encourages voice, exercise and movement, even if only foot-tapping. Community singing is always enjoyable and often provokes communication and social interaction.
- Anything that aids understanding.

### Ruby and Ivy dance the valeta

*One dramatherapy group liked to end by singing songs. One day, a client pointed out that a particular song was always used in dance halls. This led to a discussion about ballroom dancing and Ruby said that she had never managed to master the sequence of the Valeta. Ivy responded immediately by saying that she used to teach ballroom dancing to schoolgirls. She agreed to teach the Valeta during the next dramatherapy session. So Ivy utilised skills that had lain dormant for years, and Ruby acquired skills she had desired as a young woman.*

Reminiscence therapy can be fun, but it can also be emotive and the emotions it arouses can be very powerful – some pleasant, some less so. As in all their work, dramatherapists doing reminiscence therapy are particularly aware of all its aspects and are ready to deal with any feelings that arise.

### Physical exercise
Some people with whom dramatherapists work are inactive on account of their physical or mental state and need to be encouraged just to move muscles to keep them mobile. This is an appropriate function for dramatherapy and there are a number of ways (many based on the manner in which actors 'warm-up' to a performance) in which dramatherapists can promote mobility and flexibilty. Even simple activities such as tapping feet and clapping to music promote action. In order to avoid muscular damage, even the simplest of

exercises for people of restricted mobility should be performed gently and if there is any doubt about a client's ability a physiotherapist should be consulted.

It is important to do some gentle form of physical warm-up with infirm clients or those with restricted mobility before they undertake exercise. A simple ritual is to:

1   Move first a finger, followed by hand and wrist, elbow and shoulder. Repeat with other arm.
2   Move foot, then ankle, knee and hip. Repeat with other leg. It may be necessary to provide support from a partner or group circle for this.
3   Slowly move head from side to side, drop chin to chest and up the other side.
4   Relax and let yourself fall from waist to a bending position but do not touch toes. This needs to be used appropriately and is not for people who are inclined to vertigo.

Some easy exercises to improve general mobility are to:

- Walk around the room, changing pace and stride at will, avoiding collision with others.
- Walk around the room, stretching and, at first, taking up as much space as possible. Secondly to continue but to take up as small a space as possible then, thirdly, to walk around, interchanging between taking up a lot of space in the room to as little as possible.
- In a circle, holding hands for balance, stand on tip toe and stretch, then relax and touch the floor. Group members then move inwards to make a small circle and outwards to make a large circle.
- In pairs, move around the room, keeping in step. Then trying to work together without discussion, participants gradually change the movements to vary the pace, step and rhythm.

Using music, particularly marches, can assist co-ordination in movement. Spontaneous dance sometimes follows, which can be developed into both corporate and individual action. Creative ideas on the use of exercise can be woven into the play element of dramatherapy. The therapist demonstrates a movement which everyone copies, if appropriate, group members lead in turn. For example, golf movements involve balance and arm movements, reaching up to collect apples from a tree encourages stretching, balance and arm movements.

### George casts about

*A group of elderly clients were doing gentle exercises. George reluctantly participated, saying that it reminded him of his school days. The dramatherapist asked him what he did enjoy and he said 'fly-fishing of course' and demonstrated the arm movements. The rest of the group copied him, and each tried to demonstrate exercises they found enjoyable. The drama-therapist had no more problems with resistance, as sporting activities became the theme for following sessions.*

## Movement

There is a tendency to become inhibited about movement and dance as people mature. Many clients will respond to the sugges-tion of a dance/movement group by saying 'I can't dance'. This is not true – everyone has the ability to dance provided they have some mobility of limbs. Even wheelchair-bound clients can move their arms and heads. Many people, the elderly in particular, are familiar with structured dances, such as ballroom and country dancing and these have their place. There is pleasure in movement which tends to be overlooked. Movement is also a basic means of communication and can be important to the quality of life. Encouraging mobility and relaxed movement can increase the effectiveness of body language. Freedom of movement can also contribute to a feeling of vitality and well-being. Dramatherapy effectively incorporates movement exercises into its repertoire of techniques for all these reasons. The emphasis here is with the elderly or infirm but they are applicable to many other client groups. For example, boisterous young people may benefit from them. Amongst the exercises accentuating movement are:

- Each individual moving around the room in a manner that expresses their current mood. Group members are then encour-aged to change the way they are moving to reflect other moods or activities, for example walking as if they were angry, sad, happy, tired, going for a picnic or for a swim.

- Group members each imagine a favourite picture and find and demonstrate a movement that expresses the essence of that picture. They then move around the room developing their movement into a rhythm, pattern or dance.
- In pairs, one person starts a rhythmical movement, the other finds one that complements it. The pair then develop the combined movement until they can move around the room together, finding three other movements to expand the first two.
- Group members write their names in the air – as large as they can, then as small as they can. Each person then finds three letters they particularly enjoyed writing and develops the movements to form a rhythmical sequence.
- In pairs, group members agree a common task such as washing up or cleaning the floor. They then enact the task, co-ordinating with each other. They are encouraged to make their movements as large as possible until they are stretching their bodies to the fullest extent. This is followed by performing the same movements as small as possible. The pair then creates a sequence using both styles of movement.

Music can be an asset to a movement session, but should be used appropriately, for example, to create an atmosphere, to create a group dance or change the mood of the group if interest is waning. Some people find music a distraction. It can also inhibit creativity as well as enhance it. Therefore it is necessary to have clear objectives before introducing music. Depending on the group and its aims, it may be more important for the movement to be a personal expression of inner experience rather than inspired by or an interpretation of music.

## Relaxation

Although the apparent opposite of physical exercise and more focused movement relaxation is strongly related. It can also be a focus of a dramatherapy group because it too can increase flexibility as bodily tension declines. As well, it is a useful period of rest after exertion which allows mind and body to assimilate the experience of being physically active. For example, clients sometimes become very tense with the introduction of a new way of working (perhaps joining a dramatherapy group for the first time). Others may experience tension as part of their disability. Past experiences re-stimulated by a dramatherapy session can also result in tension. So, depending on the circumstances, it may be necessary or desirable to encourage relaxation as part of the dramatherapeutic process at the beginning or end of a session. Although it has a place in working with the elderly and infirm, dramatherapists use relaxation exercises with clients of many other types. For example, Clare (1998: 150–1) writes about using relaxation with a group of prisoners who were angry and tense at the start of a session. He states (1998: 51):

> Sometimes it is better to begin a session (with relaxation), rather than with a more conventional warm-up. Adrenaline and energy can be valuable, of course, but they are more so when married to an inner equilibrium, and a focused sense of strength.

As well as having physical effects and benefits, relaxation exercises can calm the mind and allow it to focus. Being aware of the strong links between mind and body, dramatherapists have approaches to relaxation making use of one for both these faculties – not only movement and stillness but the power or imagination, for example:

- Group members are asked to lie on the floor (if possible) with their eyes closed and first to tense their fingers and then to relax them. This process of tensing and relaxing muscle groups is continued systematically throughout the body. After the fingers, they are asked to relax and tense their hands and wrists, arms and shoulders (either one arm at a time or both arms together). Toes, feet and ankles, knees, thighs, hips, abdomen and backs may be similarly tensed and flexed finally turning attention to the face, neck and head until that process has extended throughout the entire body.
- Group members are invited to imagine it is a hot summer day and that they are resting in a shady spot. The dramatherapist talks them through a series of imaginative experiences in what is a kind of guided fantasy. For example, participants may be asked to feel a gentle breeze on their faces and to stretch out towards the sun and feel its warmth upon them. In response to these sensations, group members are invited to relax and let their bodies go limp.
- Group members are asked to close their eyes and breathe deeply. As they exhale, they are invited to think of things they would like to remove from their lives. As they inhale, thoughts are of things they would like to replace them. The process of continuing to breathe out the bad and breathing in the good may continue for as long as seems appropriate.

The easiest way to relax is to lie on the floor, but this may be difficult for some people with mental health and/or mobility problems, so it is important to learn muscle relaxation in other positions – sitting in a chair, for example. Even tense people can then learn to relax at home or at work, in a bus and even waiting in a queue. Music may aid relaxation where it is possible to use it.

# 6

# THE HEART OF
# DRAMATHERAPY

All the exercises described and discussed in the previous two chapters are applications of dramatherapy to a purpose. Many or all of these exercises and techniques are widely used in the training of actors as well as by dramatherapists. Also, they have a role in what may be called remedial drama (that is, the use of theatre and theatre skills as a 'corrective agent', see, for example, Thompson, 1998). In both drama training and remedial drama (and other applications) the theatre and theatre skills exercises previously described may have a therapeutic effect for those who experience them but, as indicated in the opening chapter of this book, dramatherapy has 'therapy' as its core objective. Dramatherapy is more than the application of theatre to growth, healing and learning. It is a discipline in its own right with its own techniques and processes. These are what constitute the heart of dramatherapy. What follows is an exploration of these techniques and processes.

## *The importance of 'role' in dramatherapy*

Metaphor and role are closely linked and are fundamental to dramatherapy. 'Metaphor' is the term used to describe the disguising of reality in fantasy 'as if' it were real. For example, one might say of a helpful person, 'she is an angel', or, of a mischievous child one might say 'he is an imp'. Metaphor also creates a distance from reality, and makes it easier to speak the truth and understand or tolerate a difficult situation. Landy describes this distance within a role as presenting in three ways (Landy, 1993: 25): over-distance from a role – too remote from; under-distance – too close to it; aesthetic distance is the balanced and desirable state. It is this 'aesthetic' distance that is desirable in dramatherapeutic role play.

Role, in its theatrical sense is the character adopted by an actor for a performance. In a scripted play, the playwright outlines the role in detail. Improvisation, in which there is no script but an impromptu performance, allows a freedom for the actors to define the perimeters themselves. 'Role' has other meanings too. Landy (1993: 7) describes it as 'the container of all the thoughts and feelings we have about ourselves and others in our social and imaginary worlds'. It is also a term used to describe a person's function in a particular situation. These include family roles, such as 'mother', 'sister', 'child'. Or they can describe work roles such as 'teacher', 'accountant', or social roles such as 'friend' or 'hostess'. 'Role' is also understood in terms of aspects of a person's way of being in the world more akin to 'subpersonality' (see Wilkins, 1993: 8–9) or 'configuration of self' (see Mearns and Thorne, 2000: 103–5).

'Role' is an important concept in psychodrama, which is closely related to dramatherapy. Jacob Levi Moreno, who was the creator of psychodrama, writes profusely on the subject (see Moreno, 1977: section v). Blatner and Blatner (1988b: 101–12) devote a chapter to discussion of role pointing out that 'in real life, a person is living within a complex comprised of many roles, operating on several levels of social organization and in relation to other roles' (1988b: 104). Whilst taking account of the importance of the concept of 'role' in other approaches (whatever label attaches to it), Jones (1996: 196–7) points out that:

> Within Dramatherapy, role is not confined to dramatic ways of working with role functions. It is used in its wider sense, describing a fictional identity or persona which someone can assume, and is also a concept used to understand the different aspects of a client's identity in their life as a whole. Both therapist and client can take on fictional roles during a Dramatherapy session.

Jones (1996: 197–9) goes on to point out that, in dramatherapy, there are three ways in which a dynamic tension may be set up between an enacted fictional self and a client's identity. It is this dynamic tension that is the basis for therapeutic change in role work. These three ways (after Jones) are:

1   The client assumes a fictional identity which is not their own (for example, another person, an animal or object or even an abstract quality).
2   The client plays the role of her/himself in a different time and/or place (for example, as a child, at the present time but in a different situation or projected into the future).
3   The client deliberately isolates a specific aspect of themselves or their identity, the highlighted aspect forming the basis of a created role (for example, 'mother', 'teacher' or a characteristic such as 'that part of me that wants to leave hospital').

## Role play

Action of the kinds described can be considered to fall into the category of 'role playing'. Role play is not an activity confined to dramatherapy. It is used in many ways, for example, team building and training. Yardley-Matwiejczuk (1997: 15–35) describes its use in social psychology research, clinical research, therapy and treatment and as a training tool. Role play is intrinsic to dramatherapy and has its particular uses and effects. For example, role play may be a way of exploring roles a person has in their life outside the therapy session and investigating how these are performed. Effective role performance (that is, the way in which a person conducts themselves in various aspects of their day-to-day being) is essential to the quality of life no matter how old the person may be. The number of roles people can occupy and move between usually increases with age, reaching a peak in middle years and then decreasing. It demands acceptance of the role and also the motivation and skills required to carry it through. Take, for example, the role of grandparent, acceptance of this may prove difficult if interest in small children has waned and the ability to care for them diminished through age or infirmity. Dramatherapy can help clients to increase their efficiency in current roles, relinquish roles that are no longer relevant and search for new roles. Moreno, who developed psychodrama (Wilkins, 1999: 5–12), propounded a theory of role and techniques for expanding them (Moreno, 1977: section v). Dramatherapists who are appropriately trained, have a choice when addressing role performance in their sessions – to use the psychodramatic method or to work within the boundaries of metaphor in order to explore roles and relate them to reality. By enacting roles played as fictional characters, clients can experience and reflect on a range of qualities contained in those roles. When a role is understood and appreciated, it is possible to experiment with different ways of performing it in diverse situations whilst remaining in an imagined character. Reflection on the various scenarios enacted can then help clients to understand their behaviour as it has been revealed by the role play. As indicated above, it is the experience and understanding of familiar roles exercised differently that is one of the instruments of change of dramatherapy.

### Alice's balloon is burst

*A group of dramatherapy students were looking at ways of using stories for personal exploration. They had selected their characters, and developed ways of walking and talking in role. They then suggested that each person enact a small scenario from the play or story. Alice had chosen to play Piglet from the Winnie-the-Pooh stories. She opted for the scene where Piglet sets out with a balloon to give to Eeyore, the donkey, for his birthday (Milne, 1986: 77). Piglet is so anxious to arrive before his friend Pooh that he hurries along the path, trips and bursts the balloon. He is terrified by the bang and thinks the world has exploded, or maybe just the forest, or maybe just him. When he finally overcomes his fears and reaches a sad Eeyore – who thinks everyone has forgotten his birthday – he is first to arrive, but with a deflated balloon. When Pooh arrives with an empty honey pot, having eaten the honey on the journey, it looks like a disastrous event. However, Eeyore enjoys putting the remnants of the balloon into the empty pot and the story ends happily. Alice played out this story with the aid of the rest of the group. She became tearful at the close of her performance and it was clear that some processing and reflection on the role would be helpful.*

In reflecting on what had happened, facilitated by the dramatherapist, Alice recognised four parts of herself. There was:

1   The anxious self that behaved carelessly (falling over in haste)
2   The small, timid self that was afraid of unusual events (the balloon bursting)

3   The guilty self when she upsets others (arriving with a burst balloon and witnessing Eeyore's sadness)
4   The self that could not believe in a successful outcome (even though the story ends happily)

Alice decided she would like the opportunity to revise her role as now she had the recognition and understanding resulting from reflection on her presentation available to her. The rest of the group and the dramatherapist willingly engaged with her to re-run the drama again with Alice in the role of Piglet – but this time she would be a different kind of Piglet.

### Alice and Eeyore celebrate

*Alice imaginatively re-entered the One Hundred Acre Wood, and as a different, more confident Piglet, still clutching her balloon, she began to make her way to where Eeyore could be found. This time, she re-enacted the story by walking carefully and not bursting the balloon. She then re-enacted the balloon bursting sequence, trying to be curious about the bang rather than being overwhelmed by it. Finally, Alice celebrated the happy solution made by Eeyore without feeling responsible for what had previously seemed to be a possible disaster.*

During a second period of reflection, Alice felt she had learned a lot about her roles and the way in which she performed them in real situations. She was convinced that this greater understanding would enable her to cope more effectively with possible mishaps and indeed to begin living her life more fully and richly.

However role play is enacted in dramatherapy, no matter whether real or imaginary roles are under scrutiny, it is important to de-role after a session (see below). Landy describes 'enroling' and 'de-roling' as implying the living and dying of the role. He says that:

> The actor's dilemma is not to choose between life *or* death, but to find a way to emerge into a state of being that holds life and death together, accepting the inevitable shifts in and out among several roles. The paradox of drama is to be *and* not to be, simultaneously.
> (Landy, 1993: 11)

## Improvisation

Improvisation is a form of spontaneous enactment used by actors to enhance their understanding of a situation, scenario or character. When improvisation is used in dramatherapy there may be a script or theme to initiate the action, or it may just evolve from a playful warm-up. In this form of action, there is no script or rehearsal for the scenario – the words and actions usually being produced spontaneously by the clients. Sometimes the group members divide into sub-groups and prepare their improvisation before presenting it to the rest of the group, thus offering further opportunities for insight and discussion. The dramatherapist calls upon improvisation to aid the search for understanding of self or exploration and insight into relationships and situations in the same way that the actor searches for understanding of the subject to heighten performance. Improvisation is a technique of choice when it seems that the expression of unconscious or conscious feelings is likely to be therapeutic. In a dramatherapy improvisation, the clients become characters within a given context (chosen for its relevance to the purpose or needs of the group, for example, when group members take on the roles of a family in conflict who negotiate a settlement, when there is disagreement in the group), with no script – the words and actions usually produced spontaneously and without rehearsal. Whether as a whole group activity, or a performance by sub-groups, the experience of improvisation, the roles people take and how they play them, the interactions between characters and the environment offers further opportunities for insight and discussion.

There are many possibilities for improvisation in dramatherapy and every dramatherapist and every group will have preferences. Improvisation, by its very nature, is open-ended – it cannot be known in advance where the action will be taken. So it is usually helpful if a time limit is agreed beforehand. Normally, the dramatherapist will act as timekeeper. Some of the directions a dramatherapist may give in facilitating an improvisation are:

1  'Walk around the room, concentrating on how you feel today. Develop a walk that expresses your feelings. Who could you be, walking like this? It may be a character from a play or book, or it may just be someone you invent. Give the person a name, an age, a history. Together with the other group members, change the

room into a place where action can take place, such as a river bank, a house or a shopping centre. Interact with the other people in the scene, developing your character as you meet others.'

2   'Having created a character, create a "home" for your self with chairs, props, etc. From this "home" you may go out into an improvised park, with designated areas for walking, sitting and a cafe for refreshment. You may interact with others, or pursue a solitary course. At the close of the improvisation, return to your "home" and reflect on your expedition.'

3   'Become a passenger or crew member from a shipwrecked liner. Organise yourselves to find living accommodation, a way to find food, to explore the territory in which you find yourselves and to start thinking of ways to return home. Are there inhabitants on the island? How do you communicate with them? How do you work together as a group?'

When it is presented in the form of a group activity, improvisation can develop into an exploration of, for example, group cohesion, negotiation and assertiveness as well as offering opportunities for personal insights. Stories the group members create themselves, those read from a published source or well-known to the group members may be used as the inspiration for dramatherapy improvisation. The process is for the group members to either hear the story read or told by the dramatherapist or to work with their memories of it. In either case the task of the group is to re-enact the story, perhaps recreating it into a personalised story of their own before doing so. For example, Mitchell (1994: 42–3) tells of how a group with whom he worked improvised their own version of 'The Good Samaritan'.

Improvisation of a story may be either a whole group activity where group members take on individual characters within a tale told to them and re-enact it or it may involve work in smaller groups where each small group enacts a part of the story. Following a brief rehearsal, the story is enacted, each small group adding their part in sequence. The small group exercise can add to the richness of the experience of improvisation because it allows the same characters to be played by different people in different ways. In processing and reflection, these differences can add to the understanding of the roles and so be related back to experiences outside the therapeutic space. However it is carried out, whatever the inspiration or spur, improvisation offers a powerful way to surface hidden feelings or issues and enable participants to experience dimensions of themselves that had not previously been apparent.

## *James takes an axe to the forest*

*A group of students decided to set a scene in a forest. They opted to be free to change roles at will. Some became animals, others trees, plants and rivers. They had agreed not to use words, so they explored ways of communicating in role. It was all very peaceful until James became a forester and proceeded to chop down trees, disturbing animals and blocking a river in the process. Julia and David also became foresters, Julia working destructively with James, but David tried to repair some of the damage James had created. When the allotted time was up, the therapist said that it was getting dark, when the lights were extinguished, all creatures would sleep for the night. When the lights were switched on again the improvisation would be over, and the participants would become themselves again. Following the de-roling, time was then spent confronting the powerful dynamics within the group revealed by the improvisation. With very little direction from the therapist, members of the group had begun to explore the relationships contained within it.*

## *The use of script*

Script is a rich source of narrative for dramatherapists (Jenkyns, 1996). A 'script' is the written dialogue and stage directions intended as the basis for performance. This includes not only material meant for the theatre but also that written for radio, television and the cinema. Following experience of improvisation, group members may like to work with the text of a written play with a specific plot and defined characters. Every human emotion, situation or issue can be found in a play, either explicitly or metaphorically, which can often suit the needs of the group or individual. This can be a valuable way of enabling the 'therapeutic distance' provided by metaphor that is the essential and distinguishing character of dramatherapy.

In dramatherapy, script can be used in a variety of ways. For example, the chosen play may be performed before an audience (Anderson-Warren, 1996: 108). This increases self-esteem and can be therapeutic in itself. Performance can result in renewed confidence which results in permanent change as Gertrude, a stroke victim, discovered.

### Gertrude gets into her stride

*The group consisting of elderly clients which Gertrude attended at a day centre, was performing a one-act play. Gertrude walked with the aid of a zimmer frame and was afraid to move without it. At the dress rehearsal, she said of her character, 'This woman would not walk with a zimmer, she's much stronger than I am'. To everyone's surprise, she put the frame aside and finished the performance without it. From that day she began to gain confidence in walking until she stopped using the aid altogether when walking short distances.*

A dramatherapy session using script need not involve the performance of a whole play or script or even an entire act. It could comprise the reading of a brief extract from a play, one or two pages at the most, before dividing into small groups, allocating roles and rehearsing in the groups before presenting the piece to the rest of the group. The process does not end with the performance, de-roling (an activity which assists all those involved to move out of the dramatic engagement in which they have been involved (Jones, 1996: 28)) is an important part of it. De-roling may be done through completing one or more exercises by, for example: within the dramatic space, the group members name the role they have been playing, for example, 'I am Cinderella', then move out of their performance area into the audience, acknowledging that as they move from one space to another, they are leaving the role. Once in the audience, they reclaim their own identity – 'I am not Cinderella, I am Doreen'. Further suggestions for de-roling are to found in the section entitled 'After the session'.

De-roling may be followed by discussing the experience in small groups and relating the characters to one's own life. This in turn can be followed by discussion in the whole group. When working with a script or a play, a particular scene or selected characters may be used as a basis for improvisation.

### Laughing at Grusha's Bridge

*A class of students, working in three groups, had been using a brief section of 'Caucasian Chalk Circle' by Bertholt Brecht. It was the scene where Grusha, carrying the baby in her charge, chased by hostile soldiers, comes to a broken suspension bridge and has to decide whether to risk their lives crossing the bridge or stay and be captured by the enemy. The group divided into 3 sub-groups in order to prepare an enaction. Two of the sub-groups in the class created very dramatic presentations, faithful to the text. The other sub-group presented it as a farce, creating laughter with every step of the performance. In discussion afterwards, two young women in that group said, as mothers of young children themselves, they found the decision Grusha faced was too overwhelming to contemplate, the only way they could approach the exercise was to deny the seriousness of the situation. This admission provoked further personal work for group members.*

Script may also be used 'one-to-one'. Casson (2004: 112) records that his client Gloria brought the text of *Anthony and Cleopatra* to their sessions. Together, dramatherapist and client read the script and then improvised around the role of Cleopatra with Gloria playing the Queen and him playing her servant. Casson writes:

> This enabled (Gloria) to feel a sense of dignified power and to express her wishes and feelings: the role enabled her to rehearse asserting herself and feel a dignity which, as a patient and a victim of abuse, she felt she had lost.

Script is a useful way to inspire improvisation. It can be the client's choice (as above) or the dramatherapist can select scenes that will help group members to pursue a particular theme or route towards their goal.

It is possible for people to get too close to the character they are playing, and be unclear about their real identity. Williams-Saunders (in Jenkyns, 1996: 154) describes how she, a professional actress and also a dramatherapist, became confused in rehearsal. She was playing the role of a woman who had a dual personality, one called 'Carol' and one called 'Sylvie' in 'Thursday's Child' by Daphne Thomas (Jenkyns cites this as an unpublished play script). Acting someone with a 'split mind' she momentarily lost contact with her real self and she was not sure who she was – herself, 'Carol' or 'Sylvie'. The dramatherapist directing the play led her back to reality and all was well, but it serves as a warning to be careful when dealing with vulnerable people, they sometimes find it difficult to relinquish a role. De-roling at the end of a session cannot be emphasised too strongly!

## Theatre as dramatherapy

As already stated in Chapter 1, theatre has been considered a therapeutic agent for a long time. It was in ancient Greece that it became associated with tragic drama. Aristotle wrote a treatise called *The Poetics* in which he described the factors in a tragedy that would induce a *catharsis* in the theatre audience (Butcher, 1923: 255). The events portrayed on stage were designed to bring about an emotional reaction in the audience as they identified with the characters and the story – a *catharsis* as it was termed. The release of tension which ensued was considered to be healing. The term *catharsis* is commonly used in therapy to describe an emotional reaction to the issues being considered. However, it is only in dramatherapy that theatre is used with specific therapeutic intent.

Following the use of script to stimulate improvisation, group members may like to present a theatrical performance themselves. A chosen play may be performed in front of an audience (Anderson-Warren, 2000: 108). It need not be a whole play, but just a scene that is pertinent to the actors and/or the observers. Performance in dramatherapy is a unique method of creating group cohesion, developing self-esteem and self-confidence. The performance may be produced for the benefit of the audience, the actors or both. It can produce and promote self-confidence in clients as they act in front of an audience as well as helping them to understand a variety of roles (learning from role in performance can be of a similar nature to that discussed in the previous chapter). From the audience point of view there is escapism, identification and the objective exploration of issues, all of which (separately or together) may have a therapeutic function.

The performers are rarely experienced actors (either amateur or professional) and would not appreciate harsh criticism of their acting ability. It is therefore advisable to perform to a sympathetic audience, for example, families of the group members, or staff from the unit, ward or organisation concerned. Unlike improvisation or role play where process is considered more important than accurate portrayal, performance requires the actors to perform to the highest standard the group can produce. This will vary with the clients' capabilities, mental health and therapeutic needs. As stated above, a selected and invited audience will be sympathetic to performers who are relatively inexperienced and who may be experiencing emotional or mental distress or be disabled either physically or mentally.

### Veneta goes to the ball

*Veneta was a young woman suffering from acute anxiety. She found it difficult to meet anyone and hid behind the therapist if strangers were in the room. She joined a dramatherapy group that was presenting a dance/movement display and found she was able to express herself with her body. The group produced a rehearsed improvisation based on the story of Cinderella in which Veneta took the title role. They performed before the rest of the day hospital clients and staff. Veneta's performance was loudly applauded, and she obviously enjoyed the call for 'encore' and its subsequent ovation, returning to curtsey three times. The next day she was her usual retiring self, but she was clearly pleased with her achievement and said 'I did it didn't I? Maybe I can do it again'. The performance had given her hope.*

## The audience

An alternative use of theatre is to be members of the audience. As stated earlier, theatre offers an opportunity to view issues and relationships with which clients can identify in an objective fashion. Plays or scenes can be seen for discussion by the audience, who may be either clients, or their relatives and friends or both together. For example, *Sarjeant Musgrave's Dance* by John Arden (1982) is a good representation of Post Traumatic Stress Disorder (PTSD). Langley (2004: 74–8) has written an analysis of the characters in the play relating it to his own experience as a Medical Officer in a war zone, and later as he worked on war pensions assessments. He states that 'the arts hold more for doctors than direct clinical relevance and this play is no exception', indicating that plays can be educational both to clients and their therapists alike.

Shakespeare has given us any number of characters and situations with whom to identify. Cox has described the use of *King Lear* at the British Secure Psychiatric Hospital, Broadmoor (Cox, 1992: 56). Some of the patients there identified with the characters and their circumstances and told their psychiatrist of the comparison. Plays presenting 'angry young men' such as John Osborne's *Look Back in Anger* or relationship issues – Ibsen's *Ghosts*, for example, or even ancient Greek tragedies such as *Oedipus Rex* by Sophocles – can be of value to a present-day audience.

## Creating and telling stories

Metaphor in stories has been used as a way of communicating ideas since time immemorial. Storytelling plays a part in the shamanic tradition referred to earlier as a forerunner of dramatherapy and the earliest piece of writing, the *Epic of Gilgamesh*, found on clay tablets from ancient Babylon, is a story. Stories remain an important force in some cultures. For example, in the Native Australian tradition, there is an oral tradition of transmitting sacred concepts through storytelling, thus the Warlpiri people of Central Australia tell of the *Jukurrpa* or 'Dreaming'. This is the seminal story of the creation of the world (see Napaljarri and Cataldi, 1994) and is a way of transmitting from one generation to another the necessary knowledge of traditions, places, etc. Storytelling is a similar way of 'teaching' in the Sufi tradition (see, for example, Hasan, 1998). Poetry too has been used to express and convey religious thought and feeling. Examples include *The Song of Solomon* from the Old Testament and *The Name of My Beloved* (see Singh, 1995) which contains verses of the Sikh Gurus. Wilkins (2000: 144) argues that because 'people make sense of their experience and communicate it to others by telling stories' and that 'storytelling is considered to be a fundamental way in which people make sense of our lives', 'it makes sense to use [stories] in any investigation of human experience'. The story form (as tales, plays or poetry) communicates much about human relationships. For these reasons and others, the age-old art of telling stories, although a special skill in its own right, is closely associated with dramatherapy (see, for example, Gersie and King, 1990; Gersie, 1991; Lahad, 1992). In addition, Watts (1996: 27–33) has written about 'Working with myth and story' and Meldrum (1994: 189–93) discusses storymaking as assessment.

Gersie (1997: 67) and Lahad (1992: 156) have both contributed to the theoretical understanding of storymaking as dramatherapy by proposing ways of structuring stories. Gersie's structures are:

1 the landscape
2 the character
3 the dwelling place
4 the obstacle
5 the helpmate
6 the resolution.

Gersie's clients are asked to draw or tell or act out a six-part story structured around these elements. Lahad also proposed six elements around which to structure a story. His are:

1   The main character and where that character lives
2   The mission or task that character has to fulfil
3   The person or thing that will help the main character
4   The obstacle which stands in the way of the main character completing the mission or task
5   How the character copes with the obstacle
6   What happens next – does the story end or continue?

Lahad invites his clients to draw a story board for each of these stages. Casson (2004: 100) records the effect of using Lahad's method, in the words of his client Leah:

> I liked it when John and I did an exercise together with an imaginative story: anyway this [story] did me good and my mind was refreshed after I did it, but first nervous and surprised with myself ...

In dramatherapy, stories can be used in a variety of ways:

- The story can simply be told and reflected upon
- The story can be told without an ending, which the group/client supplies
- The narrative can be enacted or form a basis for improvisation
- Groups or individuals may create their own stories, adding to the account spontaneously or formally in turn
- Enacted stories can be a useful source of group or individual exploration, frequently revealing unspoken group or personal issues.

### The dragon and the fairy

*A group of people with learning disabilities enjoyed creating stories. Monsters and scary creatures frequently figured and were greeted with shouts and demonstrations of mock fear by the group. A time came when two of the members were to be transferred to another part of the county. Everyone was upset by the pending break up of the group. The week before the end of the group, they invented a story. There were seven castaways on a desert island. They built themselves a house,*

*found food and water and lived happily. One day a dragon
came to their home and captured two of their number, flying
away over the mountains with them. That night, as the
remainder sat by their fire, a beautiful fairy came to them
and said she could take messages anywhere in the world. The
castaways asked her to go to their friends and tell them that
the seeds they had planted were growing into bushes and
would always be a reminder of their presence.*

After the story was told, responding to the metaphor, the
dramatherapist suggested that everybody posed for a group photograph. This was done and a copy of the photograph was made
for each group member. Everybody said something about the
group and this was written on everyone's copy. When the two
members being transferred left they had a tangible reminder of
their friends.

## After the session

After a dramatherapy session it is essential to bring the clients'
awareness back to the present and discuss their feelings and understanding gained by the experience. As Jones (1996: 27) notes:

> To leave a client in role or suddenly to close the dramatic activity can be
> highly problematic. It can result in role confusion or in an individual or
> group leaving in a state of identity confusion. Some sort of disengage-
> ment is usual within a Dramatherapy session.

This is effected in several ways: de-roling, reflection, discussion
and closure.

### De-roling
It is important that, as in role play, after a storytelling or making
group, clients are not left with unwanted feelings belonging to the
role they have played or that have been aroused by the activity in
which they have been engaged. Sometimes simple discussion and
reflection on the experience is sufficient to discharge these feelings, but there are a variety of expedient techniques which assist in
gaining clarity, establishing distance from the enacted role and a
resumption of personal roles and in digesting and absorbing the
effects of the enactment. Some techniques are:

- Place two chairs accessible to all, one entitled *me* and the other *role*. In turn each person sits on the *me* chair and identifies feelings and experiences that belong to them personally. Then they sit in the *role* chair and name anything that is associated with the role they have played and not with them personally.
- Place two chairs accessible to all. One is entitled *retain* and the other *discard*. In turn each person sits on the *retain* chair and names the attributes from their role they wish to retain and then the *discard* chair to name those they no longer wish to keep.
- Ask each person to imagine a casket for safe keeping in which they place the personal associations from the improvisation. The group members then imagine a rubbish container into which they pour their unwanted feelings.
- Invite each person to describe a method of disposal for their unwanted feelings (such as creating a bonfire and burning them). They then imagine a method of securing those feelings they wish to retain (such as putting them carefully into a pocket or container). These images are then enacted individually.

### Martin reclaims his gentleness

*Martin had been playing the role of a violent father who was always angry and beat his son. Whilst sitting in the 'role' chair he said that the violence belonged to the character he had been playing. He said how frightening it had been in that role to lose control of his temper. He wished to leave both the violence and the fright in the 'role' chair and not take them away with him. In the 'me' chair he said that he was in fact a gentle person who loved his own son, and would never strike him in anger. It was important for him to make the distinction between the role and reality so that he did not go away with confusing feelings.*

De-roling is in some ways the antithesis of 'warming-up' – a cooling off from the involvement with dramatic work. It may lead to reflection (see below) and thus may aid insight into habitual ways of being or lead to thoughts about how things may be done and/or experienced differently. When dealing with vulnerable clients, it is sometimes better to leave the metaphor un-interpreted and allow the revelations to remain unconscious and clients to assimilate their insight in their own time and at their own pace. Chesner (1994b: 129) points out that in dramatherapy it is not necessary for clients to apply the experience to their own lives. She writes 'dramatherapy may take place under the cover of relative darkness'. This is because belief in the advantages of working with metaphor and therapeutic distance is fundamental to dramatherapy, and is in fact the substance of its being.

### Reflection and discussion

Reflection on the dramatherapy experience facilitates healing. It is in this reflective phase that group members consider the relevance of the action they have just experienced to their own lives and understanding. This is sometimes inadvisable (see above), but the general rule is to allow time during the session for reflection. This is not to be hurried – it is wise to allow about a third of the allocated group time.

It is usually advantageous to share reflections in pairs or small groups first, it being easier to speak about feelings with one or two people rather than the whole group. This also gives time for deeper exploration and allows for clients to search for some kind of cognitive order from the experience. Depending on the nature of the group and the time available, it is sometimes beneficial to move from this preliminary sharing to reflecting on the enaction and the roles in the whole group. It is in this period of reflection that clients are likely to give expression to the connections they have made between the activity and their personal material. Jones (1996: 29) points out that in this phase 'the client can often make painful and important connections between the enactment and the issues they have brought to therapy'. It may also be a time when group process becomes the focus of discussion. In either case, material which will need to be addressed later may emerge.

Coming together as a group for a general discussion (which does not necessarily entail self-disclosure) is the final stage before closure. Although it is ostensibly an opportunity to look objectively at the process of the session, group members often share with the whole group personal feelings they have already imparted in pairs or small groups. Having once described their experience, individuals can repeat their story with more distance and further reflect on it, maybe finding other group members have had similar insights. It is also an opportunity to obtain further witnesses to a private episode, and in doing so, feel less isolated. Wilkins (1999: 5) has noted the view of Jan Costa, a British psychodramatist, that the process of giving testimony and bearing witness is important to the process of healing and this applies as much to dramatherapy as any other type of psychotherapy.

### Closure

De-roling, reflection and the discussion following on from it may be viewed as part of the process of 'closure', that is, the bringing to an end of the dramatherapy session. Closure is more than simply de-roling and reflection – it includes (and concludes) with a 'winding down' process of relaxation and/or contemplation. Jones (1996: 30–1) refers to this phase of a dramatherapy group as 'completion'. Closure usually comprises one or more structured activities and often a ritualised ending.

The process of closure is the final boundary between the therapeutic space and the outside world. Leaving a world of metaphor, engagement, activity and involvement with others can, if not handled with sensitivity, be experienced as abrupt and isolating. This would be counter-therapeutic. Creating emotional space and formalising endings allow clients to deal with this separation. To do this, there are a variety of simple activities that may be used (separately or in combination) such as:

- A brief reminder that the session is closing
- An opportunity to look outward towards the next event in the client's life
- A concluding ritual
- A reminder of the time and place of the next therapy session
- The therapist asks where the group are going next
- Each individual states his/her next move, either aloud to the group or partner, or silently to him/herself
- The group stands in a circle facing inwards. When each individual feels ready they turn to face outwards. When all are ready, the group leaves the room
- If the room is to be used for other purposes, the group clear the room and restore it to the order it was in at the beginning, then form a circle to say 'goodbye'
- The group stands in a circle and individuals just say words relating to the session, and/or state feelings they want to leave behind and/or feelings they would like to take away with them.

### Hey Ho, Hey Ho, It's Off To Lunch We Go!

*A group of people with learning disabilities had been enact-*
*ing scenes from Snow White and the Seven Dwarfs and*
*singing some of the songs from the Walt Disney film. At the*
*end of the session, they were standing in a circle holding*
*hands in closure before returning to their ward. Jimmy*
*started singing 'Hey ho hey ho it's off to work we go' when*
*Donna said 'No we're going to lunch'. Everyone laughed when*
*she sang 'Hey ho, hey ho it's off to lunch we go' and they all*
*joined in singing. This became a closing ritual, which the*
*group always sang before leaving the therapy room.*

## Conclusion

This chapter describes some of the activities that can be the heart
of a dramatherapy session. The suggestions of games and activities
are simply techniques that can be used with any group of people.
When used appropriately they become part of the therapeutic
process. Healing lies within that process and is dependent on the
relationship formed between the therapist and client combined
with the dramatic content and integration of coherence of thought
and feeling. The overall structure is common to all dramatherapy
groups but the content will vary with the needs and abilities of the
group members. There are so many dramatic and therapeutic
devices available that only brief examples are given here. It is often
the simple strategy that is most effective and spontaneous ideas
that give rise to the greatest creativity. Contributions from the
clients enhance identity with the group and encourage cohesion
within it. For, eventually it is within the therapist–client and client–
client relationship that therapy takes place.

# 7

# DRAMATHERAPY AND 'MENTAL ILLNESS'

As was made clear in Chapter 1, dramatherapy has the potential to effect change in a wide spectrum of conditions and problems if applied and conducted appropriately. In later chapters, the efficacy of dramatherapy with particular client groups (for example, prisoners, older people, children, victims of abuse) has been explored but it is also an approach of great value in working with people who suffer mental and emotional distress, sometimes of an extreme nature. Even here dramatherapy may be efficacious. In this chapter, there is an exploration of dramatherapy in the context of mental health issues and with reference to the diagnostic categories used by the medical and psychiatric professions. This is not because dramatherapy is necessarily based on the same conceptual framework but because dramatherapy is used in settings where the language of psychiatry predominates. Thus it is useful to show how the two systems may work together and how dramatherapy contributes to the healing of people with mental health problems.

## *Dramatherapy and 'healing'*

When contemplating healing, in dramatherapy, as in other fields (in this case especially psychiatry), it is useful to ask 'what or whom are we attempting to heal?'. Is it a specific disease of the mind comparable to a physical illness such as pneumonia or is it the perception or attitude of the client suffering from the effects of trauma or the perception of dis-ease (in the way of distress) from whatever cause? Disease or dysfunction of an organ/mind can and does cause dis-ease in a person – or personal illness (see below). Dis-ease is about personal feelings or a sensation that things are not as they have been in the past or as one would like them to be and dysfunction is a sign that something is not operating as in the past. In this sense, symptoms indicating dis-ease may be either long lasting or episodic, and need to be distinguished from enduring personality traits which, when amounting to personality disorder, may also cause distress to the self or others. So it is of consequence to understand the effects of the dis-ease or dysfunction at all levels.

It is also useful to have in mind some concept of health. Winnicott (1971: 6) offers one explanation as he describes a healthy life:

> characterised by fears, conflicting feelings, doubts, frustrations, as much as by the positive features. The main thing is that the man or woman feels he or she is living his or her own life, taking responsibility for action or inaction, and able to take credit for success and blame for failure. In one language it can be said that the individual has emerged from dependence to independence or autonomy.

Healing can be aimed at the:

- Removal or alleviation of symptoms such as anxiety or depression, by, for example, relaxation exercises
- Correction of (psycho) pathology, for example, resolution of conflict by dealing with denial or compulsive repetition. The metaphor of dramatherapy is important here to assist the client to be objective and present an alternative way to view the problem. This can also be dealt with by psychotherapy and/or pharmacology
- Remedy of fundamental causes, for example, coming to terms with childhood trauma. Again dramatherapy aids the clients to distance themselves from the problem.

The latter is the most demanding level and in psychiatry is the most problematic to combat.

The adequate management of people in emotional distress depends on more than just the diagnosis of disease and assessment of personality. It also includes consideration of their family, occupational and social context, their genetic endowment and personal perception of their own life story – their narrative. In this setting diagnosis is sometimes seen as too narrow a concept, but its use is analogous to the classification of books on the shelves of a library.

It is useful for general orientation, but does not preclude giving each individual book its own title and meaning.

## Dramatherapy, antipsychiatry and critical psychology

From the nineteenth century onwards, all mental health problems were termed *illnesses* and 'medical' (or more precisely biological) causes were sought. In the 1960s an antipsychiatry movement, followers of whom abhorred the categorisation of patients, came into being. R.D. Laing and Thomas Szasz were among its chief protagonists. This brought about a transfer of emphasis away from purely medical terms to include social and power issues as well. It also hastened the move away from long-term hospital treatment to care in the community. A new integrated perspective emerged which resulted in changes that had social and legal implications as well as altered terminology. The original reaction against the *medical model* as it was termed, was extreme – relating almost all psychiatric developments to professional considerations of power and prestige (Lemma, 1996: 199), but modern techniques of understanding brain function and chemistry demonstrate that there is a brain/mind continuity that cannot be ignored (Greenfield, 1997: 149, Robertson, 1999: 8). That is not to say that the broader perspectives of the 1960s are forgotten or are irrelevant to the practice of dramatherapy. Similar criticisms persist in the critical psychology of the present day. Critical psychology differs from traditional psychology in fundamental ways. For critical psychologists, mainstream psychology (including, for example, clinical psychology in its prevalent form) involves practices and norms that are said to hinder social justice to the detriment of individuals, groups and communities (see, for example, Newnes et al., 1999, 2001 and Joseph, 2003). Individual dramatherapists will vary (according to their personal beliefs and/or work settings) in the position they take with respect to these ideas. However, implicit in dramatherapy is a belief that healing is an internal and individual process facilitated by the dramatherapist through the agency of enaction.

Some radical measures such as the rapid closure of large mental hospitals (in the UK and elsewhere) have created problems for people who require long-term care or who may be a danger to themselves or others. Other reactions such as the creation of small residential units and support for vulnerable people living in the community have established a new ethos in mental health. However drastic the original movement was, the last three decades of the twentieth century saw a merging of ideas to create a more balanced view in the treatment of mental health problems. This included the establishment of drama-therapy, as part of the spectrum of treatment offered by the mental health services in the UK. It was, for example, during this period that the Arts therapies (art, drama and music) became recognised as a 'pro-fession supplementary to medicine' and that posts for dramatherapists were established in the NHS. It is partly because of this integration into mainstream mental health care that the language and techniques of psychiatry are of relevance to the practice of dramatherapy.

## Psychiatric concepts and dramatherapy

In the context of dramatherapy (certainly when working with other healthcare professionals), without wishing to 'label' *people* or deny individuality, a collective name for a group of *symptoms* (a syn-drome) is, as already noted, a useful diagnostic label which may also indicate the possible course of the illness (prognosis) and signifies potential treatments: psychiatric, dramatherapeutic or other. In order to find a widely accepted classification of symptoms, international discussions produced agreement on the grouping of characteristics to produce guidelines for the diagnosis of mental illness. The World Health Organization's Psychiatric Glossary of the International Classification of Diseases, 10th edition (ICD-10) is currently in use by the National Health Service in the UK. The Diagnostic and Statistical Manual of the American Psychiatric Association Manual (DSM-IV) is also widely used. In order to avoid pejorative terms such as *disease* and *illness*, the term *disorder* is used throughout ICD-10. Some knowledge of the broad categories of mental disorders is necessary for the understanding of these conditions for dramatherapists in order to communicate the results of therapy to other professionals involved in the care of the clients. For further information of the main categories of anxiety depressive disorder, the schizophrenias, the organic psychoses, personality disorders and drug and substance abuse, see the relevant manuals mentioned above.

In addition to diagnostic considerations in treating people, there are many additional 'systems' that need to be considered such as: personal life experiences, the family, genetic endowment and social context. Depending on the condition and context the relevance of each will need to be considered in the management of any one individual.

It is also worth remembering that physical illness can sometimes cause or contribute to psychological disorder. Goldberg and Huxley (1992: 109) describe five ways in particular by which this may occur: These are:

1   The personal meaning of physical symptoms – people can react with fear to symptoms of physical origin that carry serious implications, such as signs of a possible cancerous growth
2   As a direct consequence of physical conditions such as those resulting from neurological or hormonal diseases, for example, multiple sclerosis or thyroid deficiency
3   Multiple or persistent pains that can result in depression
4   Side effects of medication can sometimes result in depressive illness
5   Chronic physical disease, particularly if resulting in immobility or dependency.

### Personal illness

A useful concept of *personal illness* is one in which the *person* is distinguished from the *dysfunction* caused by biological disease. *People* become ill, and their *bodies* (or minds) become dysfunctional (Fulford, 1989: final Appendix). This differentiation clearly presents the individual as the prime concern when considering therapy.

Personal dysfunction, as it is frequently termed, is a change in function resulting in recognisable symptoms which have occurred at a specific time and are often transient in nature. The client or a relative can usually describe the nature of onset and progression of the illness. Some common examples of symptoms that cause clients to seek help from health professionals, including dramatherapists are:

- Depression which can range from a feeling of malaise or sadness to a deep-seated feeling of psychotic despair giving rise to suicidal thoughts
- Excessive anxiety which can vary from a general feeling of being anxious to phobias and/or an obsessive compulsion to perform certain acts to ward off impending consequences
- Eating problems which can span a wide variety of disorders from concern about weight to bulimia and life-threatening anorexia.

All these are experiences with which most people (including dramatherapists) can identify and are suffered to differing degrees by most people at some time (or times) in their lives. It is only when they reach extremes and so prevent people living their normal lives by coping in their customary roles that these behaviours can be termed symptoms of mental ill health. That is not to say that dramatherapy is an inappropriate way of dealing with depression, anxiety and eating problems of a non-pathological kind. Indeed, it may have a lot to offer.

## *Major mental disorder and dramatherapy interventions*

Dramatherapists are introduced to the issues, concepts and language of the mental health professions during their training. They will also spend some time on placement with clients in a mental health setting, so will gain a clear idea of the type of mental health problems that may need to be addressed during dramatherapy sessions. If they are already trained mental health professionals, they can opt out of the placement in favour of one which is unfamiliar to them. In a psychiatric setting, disabilities of mind and disturbance of emotion may predominate amongst dramatherapy clients. This sometimes requires usual dramatherapy techniques and practices to be modified in order to encompass or remedy them.

### *Depression*
Most people experience a depressive episode at some time in their lives. It may be brought about by bereavement or some other form of personal loss, i.e. it may be stress-related. Depression of this kind is often short-lived and does not usually require treatment (although the opportunity of exploring thoughts and feelings in a dramatherapeutic setting may be helpful). If the depressive condition persists and has a debilitating impact on function, then it can be described as an illness and therefore worthy of treatment. Depression may be classified as 'mild' or 'severe' but there is of course a complete spectrum between these extremes.

A mild depressive episode is indicated by a feeling of despondency, loss of interest, poor sleep – often waking in the early hours of the morning – loss of appetite, weight loss, low energy and fatigue over a period of more than a few weeks. A mildly depressed client usually manages to continue working and cope with usual activities, albeit with difficulty. A severe depressive episode is more intense, with the sufferer experiencing agitation, restlessness and extreme distress, usually resulting in absence from work and a slowing down of function. Sometimes the client experiences repetitive thoughts which interfere with both mind and action. There may be a tendency to repeatedly talk about thoughts, feelings or events to anyone who will listen – much as the Ancient Mariner by Coleridge, in the poem with that title. Friends, relatives and therapists may find it difficult to tolerate this frequent repetition which seems to have no purpose or resolution but which appears to reinforce the client's lack of self esteem. For example:

### Gertrude's never–ending story

*Gertrude was a middle aged woman suffering from depression. Her husband found it difficult to cope with her repetitive talk of a deprived childhood and the continued distress it caused him. Gertrude was treated as an out-patient, always arriving early for her appointment. She would tell her story to the receptionist when she reported at the desk. She then talked with the social worker, the duty nurse, and finally with anyone else in the waiting room who would listen. When she reached the psychiatrist, she would say how much better she felt just by attending the clinic!*

The confused thoughts sometimes associated with more severe depression may result in disorientation, impaired memory and disruption of ego boundaries. This furthers feelings of isolation and worthlessness and may lead to depressive pseudo-dementia. A severe depressive episode may also result in suicidal thoughts (possibly even attempted suicide) and/or psychotic symptoms often leading to admission to hospital.

Dramatherapy may be an appropriate intervention at most stages of depression. If a dramatherapy group consists of clients who are experiencing a variety of different levels of depression then it is possible that the less depressed people will have an uplifting effect on those who are more depressed. Dramatherapists are watchful to ensure that the reverse does not happen and that group and individual morale is not lowered by asking clients to perform above their current range of ability. Brief, stimulating sessions help to combat the fatigue and inertia induced by depression, whilst also taking into consideration the attendant lack of concentration.

If the dramatherapy group comprises people with the same level of depression, the aims may be more specific. For example, for people in the early stages of depression, dramatherapy can help to combat the sense of isolation and hopelessness so often experienced. If the depression has been precipitated by loss such as bereavement, divorce, physical assault or burglary then at some point it will be necessary for the client to come to terms with the situation, but the immediate need is for security, acceptance and a peaceful environment. This is a suitable task for dramatherapy by, for example, relaxation, guided fantasies in which the dramatherapist describes peaceful places and the clients relax and imagine themselves there, or even storymaking. In designing and conducting dramatherapy sessions for clients experiencing depression, dramatherapists take account of the severity, extent and duration of their clients' symptoms. Although it is in some ways an inexact categorisation and the symptomology of each client is different, it is useful to think in terms of three broad categories of depression, mild, moderate and severe and adapt dramatherapy techniques accordingly.

MILD DEPRESSION   Mild depression is usually short-lived and, although distressing, it is not totally incapacitating. Initially, the aims of a dramatherapy group for people experiencing mild depression will be to offer containment and hope to emphasise ability and raise self-esteem. Containment, for example, comes about by offering a safe place to meet with others who share similar problems without the fear of being 'odd', and form clear boundaries. An understanding of where one is, with whom, for how long, the role of staff and group members and function of the group all help with orientation. Recognition of the transitory nature of depression through, for example, discussion, the use of stories emphasising the triumph of hope over hopelessness (Snow White being poisoned by the Wicked Queen and revived by the Prince may be one such) and activities which, however temporarily raise the mood, offer a ray of hope. Emphasis on capability is by encouragement to use abilities. Physical games and movement help mobility and motivate further action. Games and exercises using thought and speech encourage mental function, such as 'I went to market and in my basket I put' where the first person names an object, the next one adds to it, and so on, each trying to remember the previous names. Confidence-building may be done by encouraging increased self-esteem and creativity and combating feelings of isolation through interaction with others – making eye contact, reciprocal acknowledgement and listening – and by games and improvisation. There may also be encouragement to pursue everyday activities and interests by discussion, preparation and support in participating in social functions.

Following an initial dramatherapy intervention, clients experiencing mild depression will probably soon enter a stage of rehabilitation where the aims of therapy are:

- Re-establishing social and communication skills
- Regaining confidence and self-esteem and dispelling any lingering guilt feelings
- Preparation for return to work and/or usual activities
- If appropriate, finding new interests and relationships.

### Sunita surfaces

*After the death of her husband, Sunita became depressed and withdrew into herself. She became reluctant to leave the house and avoided meeting other people. She was referred to a dramatherapy group which she was loath to attend. Her mother persuaded her to at least, try it out. At first, she would not join in activities, but just sat and watched. Then, one day, there was a game requiring group members to ask and answer questions. Jane asked 'In which English city is there a bull-ring?' Sunita, who had lived in Birmingham as a child, immediately answered, 'In Birmingham – but there are no bulls'. Everyone laughed and she joined in too at the thought of bullfighting in the city. The next group session focused on cities and she was able to tell the group something of her time in that city. The dramatherapy group then divided into sub-groups to produce an improvisation about the environment in which they grew up. Sunita tentatively took a small part in a scene about living in a city. The sub-groups then showed their improvisation to the other group members. Afterwards, Sunita was surprised that she could actually perform in front of others. From that day, she began to integrate with other group members and eventually she actually accepted an invitation to tea with Jane.*

MODERATE DEPRESSION   Dramatherapists tend to work at a slower pace as depression deepens. More time may be required to allow clients to talk about themselves and their problems. Lack of concentration may make some activities difficult, so simple, manageable exercises are advised. As clients recover from their depressive episode, measures of rehabilitation become appropriate.

Aims of treatment for clients with a moderate depression include those for mild depression and also to aid them in coming to terms with their somatic symptoms and offering reassurance that their depression is treatable and/or time-limited. Related to these aims is the effort to facilitate the client's acceptance of any psychotic episode that may occur and to give reassurance that it does not indicate that they 'are going mad'. Dramatherapy exercises emphasising body awareness and the confirmation of personal boundaries are particularly helpful in attaining these aims.

SEVERE DEPRESSION    Severe depression is a very disabling process. It may be necessary for people experiencing it to learn to tolerate psychotic symptoms such as a delusional belief in having committed an unforgivable sin. Reassurance that these feelings and experiences are part of the depressive illness is as important as supporting efforts to take an interest in the extrinsic events. The main aims of the dramatherapist at this time are containment of the depressed client by conveying a sense of 'holding' and security until the distressing phase passes and to provide a peaceful environment in which there is no sense of haste or urgency and no immediate pressure for the client to 'move on'. This may very well require the toleration of repetitive talk of the kind described above and constant reassurance that the current severe depressive phase will pass.

Gentle, creative activities and movement are useful to establish a peaceful environment and promote self-esteem. Tolerance and acceptance are paramount when working with severely depressed people. Medication and/or a desire to withdraw from social activities may result in clients falling asleep during the session. If this happens frequently, the therapist may discuss with the client whether to accept the sleep or try active arousal. It is also worth talking the matter over with other members of the staff team in case a change in medication is indicated. Sometimes therapists lose patience with clients who do not respond to treatment for long-term depression. It may be that the therapists reflect the hopelessness of the clients, or unconsciously blame them for not responding to treatment. It is most important for the therapist to have adequate self-awareness and professional supervision to avoid any negative transference towards the client.

When working dramatherapeutically with clients with severe depression, emphasis is on capability and the encouragement to use abilities.

Whilst the pace may be slower when working with severely depressed clients, many of the activities and aims described above as appropriate when working with less depressed clients apply to this group too. However, they have more extensive needs, for example, gentle and positive sessions with vocal exercises and movement to help to relieve tensions in body and voice are helpful. Also, group activities such as creating pictures, telling and creating stories and improvisations help to alleviate any sense of isolation. It is also helpful to use stories or images that can help clients to express feelings and find alternative perspectives on thoughts and affect, such as guided fantasies (see above) or stories about transformation such as the frog who turns into a prince when kissed by a princess.

When working dramatherapeutically with depressed clients, it is important to monitor their physical progress because it is often indicative of their mental and emotional states. For example, the amount of eye contact made by a depressed person relates to the depth of their depression. It can be a sign that the depression is lifting when clients begin to voluntarily look others in the eye. It may also be that behaviour and affect are so strongly interlinked that just as mood dictates action, so activities influence thoughts and feelings. Whatever is the case, when used sensitively, it is observable that dramatherapy activities that encourage interaction and direct contact with others help to develop the confidence and this ameliorates some of the effects of depression.

People suffering severe depression sometimes feel that life is not worth living. If during a dramatherapy session a client admits to having suicidal thoughts it is essential that these ideas are reported to someone in charge of the client's medical supervision. If possible, the client him/herself should do this as demonstrated in the vignette on p. 43. If he/she does not do this, it is part of the 'duty of care' for the dramatherapist to do so.

### Patricia makes it through the tunnel

*Patricia was a middle-aged woman who came to the dramatherapy group because she was experiencing moderate depression. The other group members were depressed women of a similar age. Patricia's depression deepened as problems arose in her family. Her daughter was going through an acrimonious divorce, her grandchild was in trouble at school and her own marriage at risk.*

*Patricia was admitted to hospital where her condition deteriorated even more. She continued to attend the group when she was able, participating as well as she could but becoming more withdrawn as the depression deepened. She admitted that coming to the group was the only time she felt less isolated. She received a variety of treatments for her illness for which she had to go to another hospital. After several weeks of therapy she finally began to respond. At this point in her recovery, she again joined the group. As the group members were talking about their states of mind, the dramatherapist suggested they each find an image to represent their feelings. Patricia saw herself in the middle of a long, dark tunnel, which was so closed-in that it was almost suffocating her, yet to take any step forward required tremendous effort. It would be easier for her to return to the darkness.*

*In the following discussion, Joan and Phoebe both admitted to having been in that situation and acknowledged the determination it would take to move forward. Over the next few weeks, Joan visited Patricia in between group sessions. Other group members offered their support, until finally the image began to change. The darkness was less appealing, the closeness more bearable and in her fantasy journey Patricia was able to take a few steps forward.*

Patricia's story shows the intensity of depression and the courage required to recover from it. Her attachment to the members of the dramatherapy group and her enthusiasm for drama as a means of viewing her situation through metaphor continued throughout her treatment. Although dramatherapy was not the only method of treatment Patricia received, it contributed to her overall understanding of herself and gave her the incentive she needed to survive.

## A disturbed sense of reality: psychosis

Whereas most people experiencing depression, however disabling, retain at least some understanding of 'reality', there is a group of mental illnesses which are characterised by profound disorder of thought (and affect). This is to such an extent that their perceptions are divorced from 'reality', a state that well people find difficult to understand. This can result in extremes of disorientation, fear and distress. Such illnesses are usually categorised as psychoses.

It is more difficult for well people to identify with the symptoms of psychosis than it is with those of depression. Although everyone dreams in their sleep and sometimes has fantasies or day-dreams and the worlds we inhabit in our dreams may be bizarre or frightening, the withdrawal of some people into an inner world of psychosis is less accessible. It is possible to dream of being someone else, or as an actor in performance, to inhabit a different role, but always there is the knowledge that this is not reality. However, persons suffering from a psychotic episode are not aware of that difference. They really believe that the fantasy life is real or that they are the person they imagine themselves to be and act upon these fixed, mistaken beliefs. It is this inability to distinguish from reality and their internal thoughts and ideas that typifies psychosis (Lemma, 1996: 156). Sometimes the fantasy life is more attractive than a much feared reality, but is still frightening and disturbing especially if, as in paranoid states, the fantasies are of being persecuted. These *delusions* are sometimes projected outwards onto other people and the client believes a particular person intends to harm them.

Whilst in a psychotic state, people sometimes hear voices in their heads. In an attempt to rationalise these *hallucinations*, clients project them onto outside forces such as their next-door neighbours or even extra-terrestrial alien forces. It is logical for clients to try to find reasons for their delusions or hallucinations but their efforts to make some sense of their experiences are usually seen by others as *non*sense. This misinterpretation can be frightening for the observer who cannot then cope with his/her own anxieties about sanity (Lemma, 1996: 18). If the spectator then projects his/her own fear on to the client, the symptoms become distorted out of all proportion. Insight or personal awareness of the abnormality of thoughts and behaviour is lost, resulting in an inability to perceive the inappropriateness of their functioning. Dramatherapy offers ways in which both voice hearers and other members of the dramatherapy groups in which they work can gain some perspective on the phenomenon and even come to terms with it. This process often eases the distress caused by hearing voices. For example:

### Lydia tells Satan what she thinks!

*Lydia was in a group of middle-aged women with a variety of symptoms. She was a religious person who thought she heard the voice of Satan at night when she was saying her prayers. Apart from anxiety about this, she showed no other signs of psychosis. It was some time before she could trust the drama-therapy group enough to talk of the voice. The dramatherapist tentatively allowed her to act a scene where she answered Satan back, and display her feelings about it. With someone in role as Satan she was able to talk more freely. Afterwards, three other people in the group confessed to hearing voices, too. There was a general discussion about it and at the next meeting Lydia reported that although the voices had not disappeared, she now recognised them as coming from within her own thoughts and not an outside force. She was more able to cope with them.*

John Casson, a dramatherapist and psychodramatist, has done extensive research on the effectiveness of dramatherapy with people who experience auditory hallucinations. He (Casson, 2004) has explored the use of drama and theatre with his client group focusing especially on survivors of abuse and those diagnosed as suffering from schizophrenia.

### Schizophrenia

Probably the most well known, but not only, psychotic illness is schizophrenia. It presents in different ways, but typically this is an extreme disorder of thought and feeling which most frequently occurs in people in their late teens or early twenties, but which may commence in middle or old age. The onset of schizophrenia may be sudden, in which case the client displays acute symptoms, or it may be insidious, gradually building up to a state where the client or relatives seek professional help. Bleuler, who coined the term schizophrenia – taken from the Greek and meaning literally *split mind* – was referring to the separation of emotions, ideas and perceptions characteristic of the illness. It is to this disassociation of faculties and the failure to operate as a whole to which the term applies and not to 'split personality' as it has been erroneously described (Lemma, 1996: 156). The consequences of this phenomenon are distorted perceptions and thoughts that can lead to inappropriate behaviour and misunderstanding. Loss of ego boundaries ensues, culminating in difficulty in discerning what is 'me' and 'not me'. It is impossible for a person suffering from schizophrenia to distinguish the inner reality from the external world, leaving an inexpressible inner turmoil. The chaos caused by the sufferer's internal splitting creates an inability to perceive things as a whole, resulting in difficulties of thought and conception which at times leads the observer to find speech incomprehensible and subsequent behaviour bizarre. To the client, his/her behaviour is logical but, as in all psychosis, leads to misinterpretation and misunderstanding by others. In addition, negative symptoms of loss of drive and interests, poor concentration and blunting of emotions are also seen. Such disturbances can be highly disruptive within a family and, when working with people with schizophrenia, it is good practice to be aware of the emotions of near relatives or others in the client's immediate circle.

There has been considerable debate about the causes of schizophrenia over recent years. There are arguments to suggest that it is a condition brought about by the effects of family and/or social environment (Grainger, 1990: 54–9), other theories favour a genetic/physical source (Farmer et al., 2005: 179). Whatever stance the dramatherapist takes should not unduly influence the treatment. Disordered thoughts and confused identity will have an effect on social relationships and it is the current relationships that are of immediate relevance to therapy, not past dysfunctional ones. Dramatherapy can work effectively and simply to enhance interaction and thus address the isolation and disconnection from the world felt by clients suffering from schizophrenia.

### From balloons to conversation

*A dramatherapy group was started for people who had suffered from schizophrenia for some years. All its members were involved in their inner worlds and did not communicate with others very much. They started the group by playing with a balloon, just hitting it to each other. This took almost the whole of the first session. The next week, the dramatherapist divided them into teams and they created a competition. Games with balloons, beanbags and balls constituted most of their sessions. After some time, the group began to talk to each other about the objects with which they played: the colour, texture etc. and gradually they began to relate to each other and talk about other things.*

ACUTE SCHIZOPHRENIA   A dramatherapist may be involved in treatment of schizophrenia during the acute stage where hallucinations, delusions, paranoia and withdrawal from reality are marked.

Disturbance of body image and intolerance of excessive stimulation may also be present. Appropriate objectives in therapy at this juncture are containment, that is the provision of a safe place where there is no compulsion to be 'normal', demonstrating and facilitating acceptance (of people as they are and the reality of their symptoms) and relieving the sense of isolation. The latter induces for the person experiencing these often terrifying symptoms, a knowledge that they are not alone with their problems. Dramatherapy will also allow the establishment of clear boundaries of time, space and person thus creating structure in a chaotic perceptual world. However, if the clients themselves are finding it difficult to cope with both the symptoms and the interactions of dramatherapy, it is more beneficial to postpone the dramatherapy till the client is ready (see rehabilitation below).

As the client is often unsure of personal boundaries and finds it difficult to relate to other people, sometimes involving others in their delusional system, the use of objects such as balloons, balls, cushions and hoops helps to focus on physical boundaries and external activities. Thought-blocking may produce problems with coherent speech making intensive verbal activities difficult. If the world of fantasy is predominant, action and actual events are more appropriate than imaginative work as it is sometimes difficult for people in this state to distinguish the difference between the reality and imagination. By paying attention to the language used by individuals it is possible for the therapist to begin to understand the thoughts and feelings that the client is trying to express. It is a difficult and complicated process to embark upon, but rewarding when successful as demonstrated by the following vignette:

### Pamela's Lost Child

*Pamela used to talk about a child in the group, she would set a seat for her and talk about her from time to time saying, for example, 'she's going to sleep now, so let's be quiet'. There was no child present but the therapist, Joanne, did not comment on Pamela's behaviour. One day Joanne was asked to escort Pamela to another venue. As they left the car that had transported them to another part of the city, Pamela became agitated that the child would get lost 'again'. Trying to make sense of this, Joanne referred to Pamela's clinical notes, which went back several years. It became clear that, at the onset of her illness, Pamela's small daughter had been taken into care, and she had not seen her since. The truth on which the delusions were based became apparent. Joanne, who had a small child herself, was able to empathise with her and begin to understand something of her delusion.*

Clients suffering from schizophrenia may be uneasy in a confined space or suffer a limited attention span, so there should be sufficient flexibility for people to leave and rejoin the group or opt out of activities at any point in the session. As there is a marked inability to concentrate, dramatherapy sessions for this client group should have a definite time limit with a maximum of an hour.

## Rehabilitation

Dramatherapy is more commonly used in the later stages of schizophrenia as a means of rehabilitation. As stated above, when the condition is acute, clients usually have enough coping with their symptoms. Clients may need to find ways of coming to terms with their experience, or there may be residual effects to which they must accustom themselves. The therapeutic goals of dramatherapy in the rehabilitation of clients with schizophrenia are to support in the transition period between experiencing extreme symptoms and a more rational sense of existence, preparation for return to a life outside the hospital and facilitating acceptance and tolerance of any limitations that may ensue from the period of illness. Confidence building, social skills and role training are all likely to play a useful part in this process.

If negative symptoms of lack of drive and motivation remain, clients will need encouragement to face independent living again. Movement, body awareness exercises and interactive games can stimulate responses. Hallucinations may still be present and it is necessary to accept them as part of daily life. In this paragraph, auditory hallucinations are discussed – they are usually induced by a schizophrenic illness. However, it is possible to have visual hallucinations (see things or people who are not there in reality) but they are usually toxic in origin. Clients can be encouraged to talk about their hallucinatory voices and perhaps have a dialogue with them as a means of finding some understanding and acceptance of their presence. In their comprehensive survey, Romme and Escher

(1993: 180–1) demonstrate that it is unhelpful for voice hearers to deny the experience, and that acceptance of the voices (and the clients themselves) is necessary to developing a successful coping strategy. They indicate that the hallucinatory voices have meaning and that discovering that meaning can help someone cope. Casson (2004) presents a detailed account of his own dramatherapy work with voice hearers which included voice work, projected play (with Babushka dolls, toy animals, buttons etc.), mask work and much more. He records that, from his research (2004: 235):

> It is possible to assert that dramatherapy and psychodrama tended to reduce voices and their impact; to change the voices so that those that remained were less aggressive and threatening; to improve people's coping ability, enabling personal change and a change of attitude towards the voices in the direction of people feeling more in control.

In general, when doing dramatherapy work with people suffering from schizophrenia, the importance of reality is indicated and an emphasis on the roles one has in life (for example, family and occupational roles) and games promoting interaction help to establish rational behaviour patterns. Therapy in groups of people with a variety of problems can help to develop communication skills and a more conventional way of relating to others. Adolescents in particular become less isolated and respond to the mutual support and assistance of group members.

When working with clients suffering from schizophrenia, as with anyone being treated medically for their mental or physical health, side effects of medication as well as the problems presented by illness need to be considered in therapy. Stimulation and action need to be balanced against the effects of over-stimulation which can be counter-therapeutic. Some clients find it difficult to concentrate on more than one stimulus at a time, so the use of music or background noise coupled with action needs to be considered carefully. It is also advisable to keep instructions brief and give only one at a time to allow for their brief attention span. Whatever one's personal opinion may be concerning the use of medication, it has to be accepted that if a client is taking prescribed drugs, then any adverse effects that cannot be controlled by dose adjustments have to be considered as part of the therapeutic process with which both client and therapist work. Modern anti-psychotic drugs, compared with older versions, have fewer undesirable side effects, but any difficulties the therapist observes during the dramatherapy session should be noted and discussed with other team members and\or therapists involved with the client. Casson (2004: 35–6) observes that a balance of medication and dramatherapy appeared to offer the best outcome with the people with whom he worked.

OTHER PSYCHOTIC STATES   Although schizophrenia is the most common cause of divorce from reality, it is possible that extreme depression, dementia, anxiety and misuse of psychoactive substances may result in a psychotic episode. The divorce from reality is similar to schizophrenia, but the condition is often short-lived. Delusions are frequently about bodily disturbances or an unjustified sense of guilt. The client reaches a state where the delusional world becomes more tangible than reality. Dramatherapy and the therapeutic distance it offers can help such clients regain a sense of proportion and reality.

### Kofi's guilt

*Kofi was deeply depressed. His daughter had left her husband for another man, and he felt it must be all his fault. Torn by this sense of guilt, he could think of nothing else. He wanted to hide in the corner and only spoke to tell people of his misdoing. In fact he had no responsibility for his daughter's actions, but his delusion cut him off from reality. After appropriate medication he was able to join the dramatherapy group and look more objectively at the situation. Through role play of family situations, he realised that the onset of his depression coincided with his daughter's marital problems which had then become a focus as the origin of his despondency.*

The Royal College of Psychiatrists (London) produces several useful booklets on such matters as bereavement and mental health problems, and information for parents on, for example, drugs (www.rcpsych.ac.uk).

## Dementia

Dementia is a condition of cognitive impairment usually occurring in old age, although some forms of dementia can occur earlier in life. Confusion and disorientation in time, place and person are frequently associated with failing memory. Perhaps the most well known cause of dementia is Alzheimer's Disease, which is a progressive disorder resulting in a gradual loss of physical and mental abilities and increasing dependency. For Alzheimer's sufferers and others experiencing dementia, stimulation is important to prolong the memory and senses as much as possible. Memory games, such as 'I went on a picnic and in my basket I put' where the group provides a list of things they would be likely to take, or reminiscence of any kind are helpful.

The onset of forgetfulness in dementia is usually gradual and the disease progresses slowly, so therapists working with clients who suffer from the condition may find themselves working with groups of people with varying abilities. As the illness becomes more severe, the individual requires more help from other people ranging from, for example, assistance in orientation such as being directed to the toilet, to being reminded at intervals to go to the toilet and at a later stage actually taken regularly to the toilet. Speech itself may become disrupted and communication difficult. As abilities are so varied, when seeking criteria for groups it is useful to consider working with people who not only have similar needs but also comparable dependency as well. A group of people with low dependency can be larger in number and have fewer therapy assistants than people with a high dependency, who may need a ratio of one therapist or helper to each client. However severe the dementia, it is still worth working in small groups of two or three clients plus assistants. When people are unable to express themselves verbally, they may still be capable of appreciating the social ethos of a group and benefit in small ways from social engagement.

Occasionally a young, physically active person may need to join a group of older, less able people creating a necessity to make allowances for varied activity. Individual movement therapy for the more active person may be indicated to supplement the group work.

### Early stages

When working with people who are confused and find verbal communication difficult, the dramatherapist's work can be facilitated by incorporating 'auxiliaries' into the group. Auxiliaries are assistants who are not dramatherapists but do have an understanding of drama. A staff drama group can inform and enthuse interested staff members and voluntary workers who have attended introductory drama courses and also drama students can be invaluable in assisting understanding and action. If the clients' comprehension and concentration is limited, helpers can reinforce explanations and instructions, assist with physical difficulties that impair movement, and generally help the clients enjoy the session.

When working with people with dementia who have low dependency needs, a group of four to eight people is advisable, but this will depend on mental and physical abilities. Group members may have short-term memory problems and difficulties in comprehension so it is advisable to give one simple instruction at a time rather than a sequence. There may be agitation and anxiety about understanding, so time is required to ensure that individuals are comfortable with any instructions. For example, waiting at the end of each instruction until satisfied that all the group members have understood, before giving the signal to commence the action. The needs of such a group are:

- Clear boundaries of time, space within the room (if appropriate) and a reminder of which room it is in which the action takes place
- Clear instructions and goals that are achievable
- An acceptance that it is safe to 'play' in this group with an understanding that the activities have therapeutic goals by explaining the relevance of each activity.

The aim of a group of people with dementia who have low dependency needs is to maintain and enhance mental and physical abilities. Strategies may include:

- Memory exercise and preservation of cognition. Just as bodily tone is improved and preserved through physical exercise so mental faculties are maintained through use. There are a number of games and exercises suitable for this purpose including 'I went to the beach, and took with me', in which the first person names an object suitable for the beach, the next person repeats it and adds another object, until all the group have added something and repeated the previous list.
- Physical exercise and body awareness work. Simple activities like touching all four walls and returning to one's chair are suitable ways of encouraging physical activity.
- Reality orientation. As explained earlier, this comprises a reminder about place, date, season, events etc., for example, by looking out of the window and noticing the time of day and season of the year.
- Maintaining social and communication skills. Simple exercises such as describing a favourite place to a partner may serve this purpose.

- Re-enforcing and validating existing roles. This is done by encouraging people to talk about everyday events and activities.
- Coming to terms with lost roles and impending dependency. This may be done by talking about change, if that is possible, or reminiscing about past events and roles. Activities that demonstrate skills such as dancing are also useful.
- Improving the quality of life. This may be achieved by encouraging creativity, motivation and socialisation. For example, the group makes a collage of pictures together or (if physically possible) links arms and walks together forming shapes such as a circle or a square, as they do so.

The latter needs to be an overall aim for all work with people who are dependent on others and/or who require long-term care. As people become more dependent, they are likely to lose the will to exert themselves. Creative activities stimulate the mind, body and emotions, facilitating a sense of achievement and raising self-esteem. Games are useful in this respect. One to encourage mobility is 'the empty chair' where the group sit in a circle with one empty chair. One person stands in the middle and the rest of the group keep moving in a circle to fill the chair. If the person in the middle reaches it first, they stay there and the person who was about to reach it goes in the middle. Another game to aid memory activation is for each person to say who they would like to be if not themselves. They can describe that person, their position in the world, and why they, the client, would like to be them. When faculties are impaired, there is a tendency to disengage from social contact with others and thus accelerate impairment of function. The more people use their faculties, the longer they will retain them and their ability to function independently.

Many dedicated people take on the responsibility of caring for people who require long-term care. Members of staff are encouraged to find ways to interest and motivate people during their daily routine, by talking to them as they hand out meals or assist in bathing, for example, or describing their journey to work or a shopping expedition. Reminders of the outside world are important to prevent clients from losing contact altogether. Dramatherapy, with its playful, non-threatening approach has an important part to play here, some ideas are given above, but always the simple activities are the best. They all provide opportunities to engage in interaction, physical movement and socialisation.

### Pauline brings the world outside inside

*Pauline was a voluntary helper who regularly assisted the dramatherapist with a group of high dependency clients. She lived in the country and had a beautiful garden. Every time she arrived for the group with something from nature – a flower, leaf, conker, stone etc. As well as helping with the session, she brought with her reminders of the world outside the institution stimulating senses, invoking memories and encouraging inter-action. 'She's like a breath of fresh air' said one client.*

### Later stages

Goals and activities for people suffering from dementia will alter as cognition deteriorates. There is always value in working with people, however disabled they become. It may not be possible to gauge the extent of comprehension or engagement, and the only achievement may be that the client makes eye contact, or shows some sign of recognition. Goals should be realistic and appropriate for people with a short attention span. Clients display their individuality and personality in their behaviour and attitude to others even when verbal communication is not possible. They can still be valued as human beings despite extreme loss of faculties.

At the highest dependency stage, one-to-one therapy is essential, whether in company of others, or alone with the therapist. Suitable goals when working with high dependency clients would be:

1   Cognitive stimulation – this may be done by talking to clients and looking for ways in which they respond, for example, showing them pictures and photographs.
2   Social contact – perhaps the best way of doing this is by working in a group setting if and when that is possible.
3   Physical movement – stretching and relaxing, moving to music and dancing are good ways of encouraging clients to be physically active.
4   Sensory stimulation – listening to music and short stories, feeling textures, smelling a variety of aromas, tasting different foods are all appropriate ways to stimulate the senses of high dependency clients.
5   Reality orientation – as with low dependency clients, this is a useful activity but often it is more helpful to pitch the activities

at a lower level. Thus, stating the time of day, name of therapist and group members, etc. may constitute sufficient activity.

6   Creating a sense of human warmth and value – simply having time for individuals, noticing their clothing and appearance, appreciating their attention and personality can be enormously important and helpful for it encourages contact and honours the human dignity of the clients.

The dramatherapist sets aside a regular period for clients to receive personal therapeutic attention, but staff who care for people suffering from dementia are usually trained to keep the above mentioned goals in mind when dealing with clients. Enthusiastic members of staff may spontaneously extend the principles of the therapy session into daily routine.

### 'Marching as to lunch'

*In order to help the people who were rather unsteady on their feet, the dramatherapist suggested walking to march time. As they were marching along, Daphne, who was a member of the Salvation Army, started singing the hymn 'Onward Christian Soldiers'. Other people joined in and the group enjoyed singing and marching together. Dora was a nurse who helped with the dramatherapy group and when the group were later walking to the dining room for lunch she started singing. The clients responded by singing and marching. This became a mealtime ritual, and other staff members commented on the way that walking into meals had become steadier and an enjoyable event.*

## Medication, mental illness and dramatherapy

Early and consistent medication is frequently prescribed for people with mental health problems as it is considered to provide consistent relief of symptoms, but this should not be to the exclusion of other psychological and social forms of treatment. As well as those intended to ameliorate long-term symptoms, other drugs may be used in the short term to combat disturbed behaviour. The advantages of medication have to be balanced against undesirable side effects, the principle ones being drowsiness, muscular stiffness, restlessness, depression and excess salivation.

Some of these feelings can also be a product of the client's particular illness and care in interpretation is required. Side effects can be minimised by adjusting the dose and taking 'antidotes'. Medication may be given by mouth, or injected at intervals of 1–3 weeks. Client responses to these remedies vary, some accept them passively or welcome the relief of symptoms, others, lacking insight into their condition, may consider medication unnecessary and refuse or forget to take their prescribed drugs.

Recently developed drugs are as effective as the older ones and have fewer side effects. They cannot as yet be given by injection so the client must remember (or be reminded) to take them. For a comprehensive account of psychotropic drugs, see The British National Formulary available in most psychiatric units and many bookshops. A small minority of clients remain resistant to most known drugs so cannot be helped by them. Dramatherapists design activities with this in mind, and act accordingly. For example:

### Vickram is misunderstood

*A dramatherapy group with people on drugs which resulted in drowsiness was enacting a scene of conflict in a family where a member of it seemed uninterested in the issue in the family. Vikram pointed out that he appeared like that in his family because of his medication. This led to a general discussion of how they were often misinterpreted and an exchange of ideas to combat it. The fact that others were affected in the same way helped them to express the problem.*

## Conclusion

Dramatherapy is an emergent and creative discipline with many styles of practice and therapeutic wisdom. The above account of dramatherapy in a psychiatric setting is a personal view and practitioners are encouraged to develop their own approaches. As observed in Chapter 1, there are as many ways of doing dramatherapy as there are dramatherapists.

# 8

# DRAMATHERAPY AND OTHER FORMS OF DISORDER OF MIND

As well as the range of disorders of thought and affect normally classified as psychoses, there are other disorders of thinking and feeling. These include personality dysfunction, situational anxiety, eating disorders and substance abuse. In this chapter, dramatherapy is described with people who are not suffering from psychosis but who are nevertheless troubled in these other ways.

## Personality dysfunction

Personality traits are habitual and persistent patterns of thought and behaviour that have been present throughout adult life and can be distinguished from episodic symptoms developed later as the result of illness. There is still much discussion about the treatability of personality dysfunction. It is not regarded as an illness because it pertains to persistent personality traits that are maladaptive in relation to the environment (Lemma, 1996: 181). Sometimes psychotic behaviour is antisocial and, particularly if it is aggressive, may present itself as if it were a personality dysfunction. Careful consideration is given to the diagnosis in order to prescribe the appropriate treatment. In a multi-axial formulation (see American Psychiatric Association, Diagnostic and Statistical Manual – DSM IV), illness and personality dysfunction are separated and may both be diagnosed in the same individual. This must be borne in mind when setting aims and assessing outcome.

### Harry adopts a label

*Harry was a young man who had assaulted a cyclist who crossed his path on the pavement because he thought the cyclist intended to harm him. His violent reaction landed him in court and he was sent to a forensic psychiatric unit where his companions were mostly drug addicts, so the dramatherapy was geared towards social rehabilitation. On discharge he again offended, but this time his reaction was associated with hearing voices. He was then sent to a psychiatric ward where the clients mainly suffered from schizophrenia and the activities were designed to cope with their symptoms. John, the dramatherapist, happened to work in both institutions. Harry's third offence took him back to the forensic unit which he seemed to prefer to the psychiatric ward. He met John again there and he greeted him with a smile and said 'I know I'm not bad because I've been diagnosed with schizophrenia.'*

Harry's story shows how sometimes it is difficult to make a clear diagnosis. However, dramatherapists work according to the needs of the group or client.

## Situational anxiety

People sometimes require help in times of crisis when the stress seems difficult to bear. It is a natural part of life that we experience anxiety at these times. It may be in response to trauma (emotional, physical, spiritual), transition of some kind or to tension at work or in family life. This can give rise to anxiety, no matter what causes the crisis. Anxiety that is clearly responsive to life events may be termed 'situational anxiety'. It is well known that crises may facilitate change as well as breakdown and so it is a propitious time for exploration. Resolutions to the issues giving rise to situational anxiety or troubles arising from it may be spontaneous, occurring with the help of family or friends, or the individual may seek help from a therapist. In this event, dramatherapy can be helpful. The prospective client may have no symptoms of disorder, but a desire to survive the crisis and solve emotional, practical or relationship problems.

### Jane becomes assertive

*Jane was a young woman who was referred for dramatherapy because of her state of high anxiety. She was concerned about her son's bullying behaviour at school and her inability to address this with either the boy himself or his teachers. Her anxiety became quite debilitating.*

*Jane had always been the 'good girl' of the family, never in trouble herself and had become self-effacing and lacking in confidence. She was intimidated by interviews with the teaching staff and unable to talk about the traumatic experience her son had suffered with her abusive husband. Her anxiety was increased when her son became abusive towards her. She was referred to dramatherapy because she was considered too inarticulate to benefit from 'talking' therapy.*

*In the dramatherapy group, Jane began to express some of her feelings through story and metaphor until she was confident enough to address some of her difficulties via role play. At first she kept in the background and did not contribute to the action. Eventually, when the dramatherapist invited her to take on a role in an improvistation of a story, she took on the role of servant in the story of Cinderella. In the reflection period at the end of the session, she said she felt the servant role was important because she was there in the kitchen and could support Cinderella when the Ugly Sisters bullied her, and she knew about being bullied, because her son had been bullied by his father, and was now a bully himself. This was the first time she had managed to tell anyone of her problem. From then on she took on fantasy roles in the dramatherapy group, until one day the dramatherapist suggested she tried scenes that could happen in reality. She was able to practice different ways of explaining the situation and asking for help. Finally she was capable of expressing herself in the real situation by requesting help for her son, whilst retaining support for herself through counselling.*

## Post Traumatic Stress Disorder

Sometimes crises or other life events are more traumatic than those giving rise to situational anxiety. In these cases there may be a recognisable and severe post-incident reaction now called 'Post Traumatic Stress Disorder' (PTSD). As its title states, PTSD is a condition precipitated by a traumatic experience such as war, disaster, rape or witnessing any distressing incident. Sometimes dealing with the survivors of disasters, such as train wrecks, fires or natural phenomena such as earthquakes, may lead to PTSD.

Although it has only recently been recognised as a disorder, there is evidence of the condition throughout history (Muss, 1991: 15–30), for example, 'shell shock' and 'battle fatigue' were almost certainly what is now described as PTSD. The intensity of the trigger event is immaterial; people can react with symptoms of stress following a minor accident as well as a major disaster. For people experiencing PTSD, events are recalled and relived in a continuous circle of remembrance. An example is described by Gersie (1997: 34) as she tells how survivors of a Los Angeles Earthquake told and retold tales of that event both to each other and anyone else who would listen. Denial and attempts to forget are rarely successful in the long term and the event continues to rankle with untimely eruptions. 'Flashbacks' and high arousal persist like a festering wound. PTSD is described by Muss (1991: 5) as 'the trauma trap'. Someone experiencing or who has experienced PTSD never totally forgets, but a situation can be reached whereby memories are no longer intrusive and feelings cease to be intensely painful. Prevention of the symptoms of PTSD is obviously better than cure. This may be achieved through 'critical incident' counselling, a systematic intervention undertaken some 48–72 hours after the event (Hodgkinson, 2000: 506), but it is never too late to commence treatment (Muss, 1991: 57).

The current method for dealing with a major traumatic incident involving several people is to hold a 'debriefing' period in which all involved have an opportunity to talk about the experience. Attention is drawn to the importance of shared narrative for people who experience a traumatic incident by both Gersie (1997: 34) and Hodgkinson (2000: 206). It is essential that critical incident intervention, or debriefing as it is often termed, is followed up usually three weeks after the initial intervention. At this time some people may need to be referred for counselling or another form of therapy as appropriate. This process may prevent the onset of PTSD or lessen the severity of it (Muss, 1991: 57). However, Hodgkinson (2000: 207) points out that the research evidence for the efficacy of debriefing is debatable and some authorities now question the need for immediate treatment (McCarthy, 2001: 167).

Not only victims of major disasters are subject to PTSD. It is recognised, for example, that people who are involved in rescues and road traffic accidents are just as prone to reactions as the individuals they are helping. Counselling is often available to police, ambulance and other rescue workers. There is also an area of training that aims to reduce the risk of PTSD amongst people whose work takes them into such stressful areas (Winn, 1994: 23).

Typical symptoms of PTSD are:

- Repeated reliving of the experience in dreams and intrusive memories or 'flashbacks'
- Emotional blunting
- Avoidance of activities and situations reminiscent of the trauma
- Bursts of fear, panic or aggression
- Insomnia
- Anxiety and depression
- Suicidal thoughts
- Excessive use of alcohol or drugs
- Occasionally, personality changes.

Anxiety and depression are common consequences of PTSD. Young and Black (Black et al., 1997: 256) recommend the use of creative therapies in bereavement counselling following trauma. In the same book, Black (1997: 285) advises the use of role play in anxiety management with adolescents who have suffered a traumatic experience, and it is also suggested as helpful in the treatment of anxiety in adults by Richards and Lovell (Black et al., 1997: 270). So elements of dramatherapy are in common usage in alleviating distress.

Symptoms of PTSD can occur immediately after the incident, weeks or months later and sometimes years after the event. When an individual has not really confronted the trauma, or perhaps denied it altogether, another occurrence stimulating similar feelings may serve as a reminder and trigger a stress reaction.

## May revisits her past

*May, a woman in her thirties, was burgled of jewellery that had been in the family for years. She felt she had lost part of her family and childhood security. Initially, she appeared to cope with her grief but after a few weeks became depressed and suicidal. During therapy she recounted an episode when she was date-raped at the age of seventeen by a fellow student. She had not complained or reported it because she felt she was responsible since she was wearing a very short and provocative dress at the time. The sense of intrusion and loss of childhood innocence she had felt then was replicated by the recent burglary, contributing to her sense of worthlessness and depression. She described the experiences several times, and created stories of burglaries and assaults, before she was able to confront her attacker in dramatic form and eventually come to terms with the events.*

The after-effects, reactions and abreactions to traumatic and deeply unpleasant events are very personal. One person may react strongly to an event that may not appear traumatic to another. For most people, the initial need is to talk about the traumatic experience. The story of the incident may be repeated again and again, but this is a vital preface to coming to terms with the event. Talking may be all that is necessary. 'Talking' can be within the remit of dramatherapy because, as Duggan and Grainger (1997: 32) and Alcock (2003: 292) indicate, such talk often calls on the power of metaphor and in this way can be called 'storytelling'.

## Donald and the runaway car

*Donald was a five-year-old boy who was briefly alone in his parents' car whilst his father was posting a letter. The car was at the bottom of a hill and another car, coming from the opposite direction went out of control before coming to a halt without causing any harm or injury, but narrowly missing Donald in the process. He did not cry but was obviously frightened by the experience. He repeatedly told his story to everyone he met, sometimes repeating it more than once to the same person. Donald carried on 'processing' the incident in this way until his fear subsided and he could at last let the incident rest.*

For people experiencing PTSD or who, because of their involvement in a traumatic incident of some kind may be susceptible to it, the primary need is to tell their story, as mentioned above, in as many ways as possible. Dramatherapy can be helpful in this process by providing opportunities for narration perhaps responding to and enriching the metaphoric element of the stories told. Other helpful dramatherapy techniques include possibly working towards enactment, not necessarily of the trauma itself, but in the improvisation of confronting the perpetrator as described in the paragraph of May's experience. Making a collage of scraps of paper and material is an alternative to painting, and the use of photographs to express feelings. They may be photographs brought in for discussion or instant pictures of group sculptures. The purpose of dramatherapy is to:

- Allow the expression of any pent up emotion and explore its origins
- Pay tribute to the deceased, even if they are unknown to the client
- Acknowledge the loss of personal well-being to any friends and relatives
- Revisit the scene or grave – either in reality or an improvised scene
- Empower the client, rectifying the sense of impotency produced by the incident
- Allocate responsibility – an acknowledgement that the client was not responsible for the event, or if s/he was, to accept the fact and work towards self-forgiveness.

Therapy should be client-led, allowing people to work at their own pace. It may be that the initial phase of storytelling lasts for a long period before the client is ready to move on. As indicated above, telling the story may be all that is needed. However, there may be emotional blocks that need to be explored before the client can progress. For example, Winn (1994: 40) has stated in her book on dramatherapy and PTSD that sometimes the expression of anger and the identification of its source is problematic. Whatever the individual's rhythm, the process must take its course and cannot be hurried. Nowadays counselling is usually available following a trauma, but sometimes the stress is repressed for a very long time and a therapist may be asked to work with people whose symptoms have only just been recognised. PTSD may become a chronic condition, for example, some veterans of the 1914–18 war still have 'flashbacks' and nightmares that have continued throughout their lives.

PTSD often stems from a relatively recent stressful situation or event but a previous history of psychiatric disturbance does not rule out the diagnosis of Post Traumatic Stress Disorder. Recurrence of an earlier mental disorder could be precipitated by the stress and would complicate both diagnosis and treatment. As noted above, casualties of traumatic events are not the only victims of PTSD. Sometimes the rescuers suffer from their experience.

'Debriefing', as it is called, is still available for all rescue services and the armed forces despite the question surrounding it. Allowing time and space to recount the experience is considered helpful to validate the individual's reaction, and put it into perspective. Dramatherapy can be a valuable means of facilitating the expression of feelings and exploration of the experience by enactment, story and metaphor (Winn, 1994: 38–44).

## Eating disorders

The term 'eating disorders' covers two specific conditions – anorexia nervosa and bulimia nervosa and, increasingly, a third form of compulsive eating which may or may not be of psychological origin. However, any eating problem, such as overeating or excessive dieting associated with psychological disturbance may bring clients to dramatherapy. Clients with an eating disorder often have either a distorted image of their own bodies or are preoccupied with size and shape. Jones points out that a valuable function of dramatherapy is that it can be used as a vehicle through which to explore the relationship clients have with their bodies 'in terms of problematic memories and experiences with which their physical self connects' (Jones, 1996: 164).

Dramatherapy is a valuable medium in the treatment of eating disorders. In particular the use of body awareness, movement and emotional distancing can be advantageous in therapy.

# 9

# OTHER CLIENT GROUPS
# AND DRAMATHERAPY

In the last two chapters, dramatherapy is shown as a valuable medium for working with people who are chronically ill or acutely disturbed. Most of them have been diagnosed as 'ill' and their problems are described as part of their 'illness'. Dramatherapy is also used effectively with a variety of client groups who are not defined by 'illness'. They are healthy people who are grouped together by circumstances, such as age (children and older people) or may be their situation (offenders) or by ways in which they are limited, for example, people with learning difficulties or physical impairment.

In all dramatherapy groups, as with most psychotherapy, it is important to establish and maintain secure boundaries such as time, space, confidentiality and therapeutic distance. Dramatherapists work with a variety of creative approaches which use the metaphorical distance provided by drama, such as:

- Storytelling – both creating stories and using myths, legends, well known favourites and fairy stories
- Pictures – painting and drawing them or using other people's pictures to express events, feelings or needs
- Puppets – again for expression and storytelling
- Toys and other objects – in the same way as a sand tray containing models of people, animals, trees, houses, etc. to create stories and scenes
- Drama – using appropriate written plays or improvising around a scene

- Role play of real situations
- Performance either to the dramatherapy group or an invited audience.

As indicated in the introduction to the section, each client group has its own characteristics. In this chapter, there is an exploration of these features for a range of client groups. It is not meant to be comprehensive but demonstrates that valuable dramatherapeutic work is being done with clients who fall into other categories. The field of dramatherapy is constantly expanding but this chapter is intended only as a guide to demonstrate how dramatherapy may be applied outside the field of mental health problems.

## Possible consequences of abuse in childhood

People who have been abused as children often carry the mental, emotional, physical and spiritual consequences of this abuse into adulthood. It may have been sexual, physical, emotional or some combination of these. Dramatherapy works through 'therapeutic distance' and is therefore a way of working with the after effects of childhood abuse without re-traumatising the client. Casson (2004) gives many examples of working dramatherapeutically with the consequences of childhood abuse in his book. Jones describes a case example illustrating the use of masks when working with a client who had been sexually and physically abused by her father (Jones, 1966: 1–3). Both indicate the power and the value of dramatherapy with clients who face this difficulty.

Playtherapists usually deal with the immediate effects of abuse in children but Bannister (1997: 54) shows that there is also a place for dramatherapy. Cattanach (1996: 140) points out that adults often want to explore the same themes as children and that techniques from playtherapy and dramatherapy with children can also be used within adult dramatherapy. Although there are similarities between the effects of various kinds of abuse, it is useful to consider the major categories of abuse separately.

### Sexual abuse
Dramatherapists are frequently asked to work with clients who have been abused either as children or later in adulthood. Some-times the trauma of abuse is repressed and not remembered until

something touches off a memory. When there is a vague recollection, a sense that something happened but no definite, concrete recall, it can be very disturbing to the client. It is important for the therapist to be supportive at such times, even when there is little actual evidence. Clients may not ever have been able to recount the experience to anyone else in the past, or may have been disbelieved if they did. It is vital to respect their client's perception, fear, doubt, speculation and emotions at such times.

When working with people who have been sexually abused, the therapeutic process takes place over a long period, allowing clients to lead it, and work at their own pace. The memories may be painful and upsetting for clients and care is taken to avoid replicating the abuse, even in small ways. If, in an action of some kind, it is necessary for someone to take on the role of the abuser, it should only be to enable clients to say things that they have not been able previously to express adequately to the abuser. It is safer, at first, to use a cushion or other artefact until it is clear that clients are able to face their abusers. Bannister (1998: 45–6) explains why it may be unwise and unnecessary for someone who has been abused to take on the role of the abuser in an enactment. She goes on to give some guidelines as to when it is important to have a re-enactment of abuse and how this may be done safely (1998: 47–8). Sanderson (1990) has written a book on working with 'adult survivors'. It is recommended reading for anyone interested in working with this client group.

Clients who have been sexually abused require specialised treatment. Therapy with children is a separate issue, but, as indicated above, there are similarities because the source of trauma and disturbance is the same, whether recent or in the past. Clients for whom sexual abuse is an issue tend to present this abuse in one of three ways. These are:

1   Abuse that happened some time ago and has been repressed from consciousness. 'Forgotten abuse' may be recalled in varying degrees, from distant dream-like memories to vivid flashes of remembrance and/or full recollection of events.
2   Past abuse that has not been forgotten, but is now being openly acknowledged.
3   Abuse of recent origin with conscious insight into the damage caused by the event/s, which may contain elements of PTSD.

In some respects there are similarities between the after effects of sexual abuse and PTSD but, as Finkelhor (1988: 67) points out, PTSD is about events and sexual abuse is about relationships. In working with children, he presents a model of symptoms that contains four 'Traumagenic Dynamics' which need to be considered in therapy. They are:

1   Traumatic sexualisation in which the child becomes preoccupied with sex and may become promiscuous, aggressive and bullying
2   Betrayal which leads to mistrust and impaired judgement in adult relationships
3   Stigmatisation leading to feelings of isolation and low self-esteem
4   Powerlessness which can lead to depression and/or self-harm or which can be counteracted by a desire to dominate others.

These are considered to be ongoing processes that require attention however recent or distant the abuse may be. Adult survivors of child sexual abuse tend to recount a number of universally recurrent themes during therapy (Sanderson, 1990: 191). These echo Finkelhor's model, including negative self-image, guilt and shame, unresolved anger towards the abuser and fear of intimacy. The two notions together give a useful guideline for client needs:

* Secure, defined boundaries
* Trustworthy relationships
* Reassurance of personal worthiness
* Expression of grief and anger
* Restoration of personal power
* Assurance that they are not to blame for the abuse
* Clarification of relationships
* Learning new roles and ways of relating to people.

These are some of the factors that dramatherapists face when working with clients who have been abused. All clients may not have all these needs, but they present an overall picture of difficulties to be overcome. There is no prescribed way of working, just a need for dramatherapists to be aware of the clients' vulnerability and work at their pace and according to their stage of recovery. The final stage is usually role play but this should only be used when clients are ready to deal with reality.

Children who are abused find ways to please or pacify their abusers. This, in turn, sets up a pattern of relating to others that may have repercussions in later life, and result in their continuing to form relationships in which they will be abused. Some children cope by dissociating from the experience or pretending it is not happening to them and this denial can remain with them in adulthood.

### Physical and emotional abuse

Physical and emotional abuse can have just as deep-rooted effects as sexual abuse and create similar symptoms and behaviour patterns. If the abuse has been continued through childhood, then coping strategies have been developed that continue into adulthood. They may no longer be appropriate or useful, but persist until the client finds new ways of relating to people or reacting to situations.

### Diane becomes invisible

*Diane had lived all her childhood with a drunken, violent father. She frequently witnessed him hitting her mother and sometimes he turned on her. When she heard him coming home, she would know by the noise he made on entry if he was drunk or not. When he was sober he would take her on his knee and tell her stories and she loved these times with him. When he was drunk, however, she would try to avoid him. If this was impossible, she would stand against the wall and try to make herself invisible. She would 'freeze' like a frightened animal, but in doing so she was often forced to witness her father's brutal attacks on her mother. The pattern of 'freezing' persisted into adulthood. If she found herself in any difficult situation she would try not to be seen even though the reaction had ceased to be useful to her. After many months of dramatherapy she could understand her motives, but the urge to 'freeze' still remained with her.*

## Dramatherapy with older people

Older people are not necessarily limited by age or disability, but dramatherapy can supply ways of maintaining and promoting physical, mental and emotional well-being. For example, dramatherapists are often asked to work with elderly people in a residential or day care setting. Such dramatherapy groups are usually aimed at improving quality of life and enhancing communication. As people grow older, there is a natural physical slowing down, choice becomes more difficult and activities take longer. Memory is less sharp and people may even forget where they have put possessions. Hearing and sight may deteriorate making conversation difficult. Occasional dizziness and loss of balance can cause anxiety and fear of falling.

All these normal phenomena can result in a tendency to be less self-assured, to withdraw into oneself and to avoid social contact. Familiar roles may be lost when people retire from salaried work, children leave home and/or partners die. Family relationships alter with ageing, for example, a mother may seek assistance from a daughter when shopping is difficult, or advice on technical matters from a son. New gadgets are often difficult to understand and younger people who are more familiar with technology may offer advice. The process of consultation may eventually lead to role reversal, where the child takes on the caring role. This may evolve gradually over a long time requiring adaptation on both sides with the possibility of contention if one or both are reluctant to accept the change. However slight the dependency, change does occur and may need to be addressed within the dramatherapy group. It is important to come to terms with the results of ageing and also create new roles and interests in order to retain self-esteem and feel valued by oneself and others. Old age is also a time to consider one's life achievements so memories become more important. Repetitive reminiscence can be difficult for relatives to tolerate, but it is part of the process of evaluating and reviewing life. Drama activities that encourage creativity, spontaneity, movement, inter-action and/or stimulate memory are invaluable for keeping mind and body active and adjusting to physical, emotional and environmental changes.

### *May dances her way to happiness*

*A group of elderly clients at a day centre were preparing a concert. They selected songs to sing solo and in groups. Annie, Louise, Hannah and Florence were practising 'When the red red robin goes bob bob bobbin' along'. As they sang, other people in the room were tapping feet and clapping to the rhythm. 'I wish we could do a little dance', said Annie. The dramatherapist devised a simple movement sequence which they began to rehearse. May, who, following a stroke, walked with the aid of a stick said wistfully that she had always wanted to be part of a song and dance act, but had never been on a stage in her life, and now could not walk unaided. The dramatherapist re-choreographed the sequence so that the group linked arms and she suggested that May stood in the centre of the group and, supported by the others she was able to move with them. The dance was a great success, and May's son, who came to the performance, was delighted with his mother's achievement, and so was she. Despite her increasing dependency she had found a new role – that of performer, and as movement became even more difficult for her, she still led the group in song.*

Dramatherapy activities for groups of older people will normally include:

- Physical action – simple exercises that can be performed whilst seated, more active games like team games, passing the ball to each other and trying to keep it with the same team, or even ballroom dancing
- Validating and encouraging a spirit of play – by showing that playfulness can still be fun no matter what the age of the participants.
- Interaction and communication – by games such as describing an object whilst the rest of the dramatherapy group tries to guess its name
- Reminiscence and life review – by showing old photographs, discussions on past activities, performances by professional theatre companies (see Langley and Langley, 1983: 142–55)
- Coming to terms with loss of roles – finding new roles within dramatherapy activities (see the above vignette)
- Validating current roles and encouraging new ones – by reassuring and motivating any new venture during the dramatherapy session
- Adjusting to any disability – by encouraging movements that can be achieved
- Adjusting to environmental changes – by reassurance and relating to other dramatherapy group members in similar circumstances.

When planning sessions for this client group, it is advisable to bear in mind the usual ageing process, avoiding activities that involve sudden movements and keeping head movements, swaying and stooping to the minimum to prevent giddiness. Physical safety is important and support should always be nearby. This could be either conveniently placed stable furniture or by the presence of additional staff members. Hearing difficulties are often experienced by older people and it is a good plan to stand facing the person you are addressing and never behind them. This allows for lip reading if necessary. Likewise sight is often impaired so facing people, standing near and even wearing the same perfume regularly, help them to identify you.

In all dramatherapy sessions licence to play is necessary from the outset of the group or one-to-one activity. Older people may regard play as something belonging to childhood and even find it demeaning. If this happens, the dramatherapist's first task is to reassure people of its purpose and introduce a sense of playfulness and fun into the group. People who are reluctant to participate initially, may not be familiar with imaginative play and games and need encouragement and explanation from the outset. Playing games played as children is not being childish, but re-creating a familiar experience to be of value in the here and now, whether for exercise, motor skills, validating memories or just for fun – provided the therapist presents the activity in an adult fashion. As with all therapy, the client–therapist relationship is of vital importance and must be based on mutual respect.

### 'Thanks for the memory'

*A dramatherapist was preparing an improvised theatre project with some residents in a sheltered accommodation complex. The intention was to produce a short Christmas entertainment for the other residents. She initially asked for interesting experiences and many were recounted. Inevitably wartime experiences were included, many of which were amusing and could become theatrical scenes. When asked to put their stories into action, the residents were united in their reluctance. 'We've enjoyed talking about ourselves, but it's not interesting for other people. We'd rather sing some Music Hall songs' they said. So they put on a lively and amusing show of songs, jokes and sketches which was enjoyed by actors and audience alike.*

*On reflection, the therapist realised that enactment may have restimulated the pain which was disguised by the humour of their stories and they may not wish to share the personal nature of their experiences with a wider audience. It was important to respect the deeper influence of their storytelling.*

## Dramatherapy and people with learning difficulties

Dramatherapy has had a valuable role to play in working with people with learning difficulties since its inception. It is not intended to be 'curative' but to facilitate optimal function for the clients in everyday activities. The broad category of learning difficulties covers a range of handicaps from dyslexia to scholastic problems, slow learning to brain damage, speech disorders to autism, restlessness to attention deficit syndrome and Asperger's syndrome. Dramatherapy is a particularly appropriate approach for these clients because so much is or can be 'non-verbal'. It is also very suitable for people with learning difficulties. Chesner (1994a: 73) takes the view that dramatherapy is in a good position to challenge the institutionalised culture experienced by many people who are in residential care. She also points out the importance of a firm grounding in the concrete and the 'here and now' before moving to imaginative dramatherapy work, but, she adds, when this happens 'worlds of possibility unfold'.

As with all clients, the nature of the dramatherapeutic activities depends on the nature and severity of their limitations. Difficulties may be considered 'mild', 'moderate' or 'profound'. Some clients in this group may experience multiple difficulties and this affects their therapeutic needs. Dramatherapists plan their activities according to those needs.

### Mild difficulties

Many clients who have mild learning difficulties come to therapy in order to develop practical and social skills and to intensify both the experience and quality of their lives. A primary task for the dramatherapist may be to re-introduce fun and playfulness into the lives of many adult clients. This is particularly relevant for people with learning difficulties. Cattanach (1996: 89) states:

> For those who have learning difficulties of whatever kind much time is spent by those who care in exhorting them to be responsible and sometimes this external pressure to achieve some kind of independence makes people with learning difficulties afraid to play and have fun. In drama, players can get in touch with their capacity to play and it is always surprising how much independence can be learnt through play and how much skill in social interaction has to be achieved if the group are to play together.

The needs of people with mild learning difficulties who may benefit from dramatherapy could possibly include:

- Clear boundaries – some such clients cannot understand the need to provide distance between themselves and others. This can result in unsociable and impolite behaviour towards other people
- Social skills training – they may need to learn appropriate behaviour in social and work situations
- An opportunity to play in a supportive environment – as Cattanach indicates above, there is often pressure put upon people with learning difficulties to conform to rigid social behaviour patterns
- Movement – There is sometimes a poor limb co-ordination that complicates activities but practice can give clients better control of limbs
- Exploration of situations – an opportunity to make and explore mistakes they may have made in social situations
- Self advocacy – how to make choices and express themselves verbally
- Role training – in order to prepare themselves adequately for social and work situations
- Self confidence and self-esteem.

The pressures on this client group can be weighty and confusing. Some individuals may be ill-equipped, because of their difficulties, to cope with sensitive interpersonal situations at work and misunderstandings can arise even in sheltered workplaces. Opportunities are given for them to make choices in sheltered workshops but they may need some guidance in order to do so. 'How do we make ourselves heard and get our needs met?' is a question posed by some people with learning difficulties. Others may feel the same but be unable to verbalise it.

Society plays lip service to equality of opportunity but does not necessarily recognise the need to learn how to gain it. There are some members of society who do understand and treat people with learning difficulties as equals and encourage them in what they can do. Others seem not to understand their abilities and focus only on the difficulties. Experience of misunderstanding and the inability to rectify it, coupled with the frustration of their own limitations can result in unresolved conflicts, anger and resentment. The dramatherapy group is an excellent forum for the exploration of feelings and personal development.

### Moderate difficulties

Clients with moderate learning difficulties may have similar needs to those with mild difficulties but at a different level. For example, it may take longer for them to grasp the implications of personal choice and ways of making personal needs known. The choices may be elementary such as choosing clothes to wear or selecting food from the menu but it is still helpful to learn to express likes and dislikes and to have an opinion about the appropriateness of clothing. Learning can be made fun by inventing games such as:

- Describing the weather and selecting suitable clothes for it – waterproofs in the rain, a broad-brimmed hat when it is sunny.
- Creating stories containing decisions which the clients can make such as a story where a character has to choose between travel by bus with their friend or alone on the train, and if the clients decide the ending this is also fun.
- Role playing experimenting with ways of expression, where the client takes on the role of a willing helper, then changes to an unwilling one, for example.

As emphasised above, a strength of dramatherapy is that it is not necessarily a verbal modality, thus people whose verbal communication is limited can make presentations by drawing, using objects or the sand tray to indicate their individual preferences.

Some needs of people with moderate learning difficulties are:

- Clear boundaries – of time and space, personal space, not intruding on others' space
- Movement – they may be physically impaired, possibly from birth trauma, learn to use abilities and not focus on difficulties
- Recognition of the right to choose
- Learning how to make choices
- Sensory experiences for recognition, exploration and development, such as feeling different textures and recognising them, seeing pictures depicting events and smelling an assortment of scents to be able to recognise them
- Basic social skill-learning to share and relate to others, respecting their needs
- Learning means of communication and self-expression such as drawing or creating hand signals.

### Robin says it with a glance

*Robin was a young man who had difficulties in communicating with others. He would get very frustrated and upset when he could not make himself understood. One day the dramatherapy group were passing a ball around the circle and naming people and he found that he could communicate intention by using his eyes and looking directly at the person to whom he was throwing the ball, when the others realised what he was doing they responded by also watching him and each other. Members of staff learned that when he looked directly at them and they waited long enough, he could find the right words.*

Dramatherapy with people with moderate learning difficulties offers an opportunity for learning self-expression, self-advocacy, self-control and developing self-esteem. The clients may never lead independent lives but can discover ways of functioning effectively within a sheltered environment.

### Profound or multiple difficulties
It is useful to remember that clients with profound disabilities, unlike elderly people with dementia, may have lived with their disability most of their lives. They are not dealing with new problems and limitations, so impeded physical activities and difficulties in comprehension are unlikely to be new to them. The physical dependency and communication difficulties experienced by people with profound learning difficulties do not necessarily mean that they are without any awareness of their environment. Dramatherapists need to keep in mind and take account of the fact that people with such limitations remain human beings with feelings and personalities of their own however disabled they may be. As such they are worthy of respect and the right to self-determination. Dramatherapy is a valuable way of facilitating autonomy, enhancing skills and aiding communication.

Although it may be necessary to work one-to-one with people with profound or multiple difficulties, it is still important to meet in a small group of two or three people wherever possible. This is because it is stimulating for people with profound difficulties to be with others and it reduces the sense of isolation that sometimes surrounds people needing constant care. Dramatherapy is dependent on the inherent creative ability of both therapist and client to be effective. This can stem from any change in environment however minimal it may appear. For example, people who spend all their time in wheelchairs may appreciate being lifted from them to lie on the floor in a different position and so to view the room from another perspective. Of course, such an activity and any other involving physical movements must be undertaken with the co-operation of care staff who know about the physical condition of the client and can advise on appropriateness of the activity. When working dramatherapeutically with this client group, it is important to ensure a balance between activity and restfulness. As well as for stimulation, there is a need for periods of inactivity – 'just being'. Swinging in a hammock can be very relaxing as can watching fish swim in a fish tank. These are the kind of restful activity we all enjoy which is a reminder of the similarities between those who are disturbed or limited in some way, and their therapists and carers.

Some needs of clients with profound or multiple difficulties are:

- Relaxation – clients can feel stressed by their environment. Suitable exercises for relaxation are those we might select for ourselves, like stretching and relaxing arm and leg muscles, if that is possible, listening to quiet music, watching the birds feeding or looking at the fish swimming in the fish tank.
- Sensory stimulation – dramatherapy allows clients with profound learning difficulties to hear sounds including different voices, recordings of waves on the shore, music and birdsongs. It also allows them to touch a variety of textures. People who are limited in their ability to move can feel cloth of various kinds and be introduced to scents and odours.
- To experience touch that is not about clinical caring – for example, gentle massage and stroking of hands, feet, head or neck.
- Exploring boundaries – how near are the perimeters of the room, who else is in the room with you, how far you can see when you look out of the window.
- Creative experiences – drawing, if it is possible, making collages, if only to point to the place you would like the material object put, and for someone else to glue it in position.
- Exploring ways of communicating – by gesture, copying movements such as clapping or sounds such as humming.
- Gentle movement – such as moving arms, tapping feet, nodding head.

Sometimes clients with profound difficulties do not appear to show any creativity for themselves and it is necessary for the therapist to provide the creative initiative in order to stimulate the client's own imagination. A spark of creativity in a group cannot fail to engender inventiveness in others. For example, if the therapist starts singing or humming, others are likely to join in or tap their feet or clap and if the therapist draws a picture, it encourages clients to attempt to do the same, or at least comment on the drawing. Any new experience (in particular changes in the environment) may generate an interest and so dramatherapy can deliberately build in new and different experiences.

### The transforming journey

*A dramatherapist working in a unit for severely disabled people enlisted the help of other members of staff to create a different environment for his clients. They decorated the drama studio, corridor and sitting room with materials and pictures. Wheelchairs were also decorated and clients then taken on a sensory journey of sight, sound and touch, through decorated corridors, rooms with a variety of materials they could feel and flowers they could smell. The helpers guided them throughout, assisting them with anything they found difficult. It was an opportunity to see their surroundings from a totally different perspective.*

As well as in the ways indicated above, it is possible to stimulate people with profound difficulties through telling and creating stories. The stories may be very simple and spontaneously created or favourite tales. Cattanach (1996: 153) recommends choosing stories with repetition and rhythmic sections and picture books with strong colours. She writes 'even if the receiver of the story can't understand, the tone of voice and the vitality of the speaker/ reader establishes a rapport'.

Unlike people with dementia, who may have similar physical and comprehension problems and who have a history of a different life style, people with multiple difficulties may have lived in a clinical setting for most or all of their lives. Imagination provoked by stories will not necessarily arouse memories but it may stimulate some inner source of creative response – maybe spiritual in origin rather than cognitive or emotional. The dramatherapist may see a response – perhaps simply the flutter of an eyelid or a faint smile. This is not a client group where one expects dramatic results, just minimal reactions to activities. Any action that shows the clients' awareness could be similar to the deep insights of more responsive clients – both show that dramatherapy is having some effect.

### Clara sees the sun

*A dramatherapist and helpers were creating patterns of light with torches in a group of people with multiple disabilities. Clara, who usually seemed uninterested in her surroundings said 'It's like the sun'. It may appear a casual remark, but for Clara it was a verbally expressed observation indicating her level of involvement and creativity.*

## Dramatherapy with children

Drama, with its roots in play, is an excellent medium for therapy with children. As was pointed out earlier in this book, Peter Slade (1995: 15) recognised the significance of play and it was the origin of his work. Richard Courtney, who was one of the early drama therapists in the USA, based his work on drama as a means of learning and personal development (Courtney, 1986: 2). There is a close alliance between dramatherapy and playtherapy when working with children. Similar methods may be used and the two are interchangeable. A number of dramatherapists in the UK are also qualified playtherapists. Bannister (1997: 8) points out that, at least in the UK, playtherapy has its roots in dramatherapy developing from it in the latter part of the twentieth century.

When working dramatherapeutically with children, the emphasis is on play and not its metaphoric significance. Jones (1996: 171) lists the 'important play areas of dramatherapy'. These are:

- Play as a way of learning about and exploring reality
- Play as a special state with particular relationships to time, space and everyday rules and boundaries
- Play having a symbolic relationship in relation to an individual's life experiences

- Play as a means of dealing with difficult or traumatic experiences
- Play's relationship to an individual's cognitive, social and emotional development
- Play's connection to drama as a part of a developmental continuum.

The link between these aspects of play when working with children are perhaps self-evident. For example, learning about and exploring reality is important in any child's life and using play as a way of coming to terms with a traumatic experience offers the opportunity of a familiar and non-threatening means of expression. There may never be a conscious association with real life as there is in the reflective phase of dramatherapy with adults, although the therapy remains in the dramatic metaphor. As many of the children who are sent for therapy have been abused either sexually, physically or emotionally, it is essential for therapists to ensure that their own behaviour does not provoke a negative response. Participation is frequently necessary, but not to be undertaken lightly. Cattanach (1994c: 103) states, 'It is dangerous for the therapist playing with young children, to jump into a role without preparation, or to play a role not clearly fictionalised'.

As with adult dramatherapy, the session may be structured by the therapist or child led (Gil, 1991: 36). Anne Bannister (1997: 40) gives a good account of the effects of child abuse in her book about the use of both psychodrama and dramatherapy.

Whereas a playtherapist is more likely to use toys and objects in projected play in which the child is inactive, using mental processes rather than physical action (Slade, 1954: 30), dramatherapists often work individually with children maintaining the personal nature of the metaphor. When working with children, the dramatherapist may use:

- A sand tray containing models of people, animals, trees, houses etc. to create stories and scenes
- Glove puppets, dolls, toys and even marionettes to represent people, animals or anything/body else, to dramatise stories and events
- Storytelling and storymaking
- Dramatisation by 'play acting'.

All the above are really about the children expressing themselves metaphorically either by invented stories or thought relating real life events. All activities can be either led by the child or introduced by the dramatherapist, but it is the child's decision to participate in them.

A child may take on roles and also allocate them to the therapist – 'You be the monster today and I'll fight you'. Power issues are as important to children as they are to adults. They need to understand how the abuse of power has damaged them before they can find new ways of coping with their feelings of inadequacy. Bannister (1997: 125) explores these issues in her book, emphasising that abused children 'need to understand how the issue of power affected them so that they were unable to respond to the abuse in any assertive way'.

Some needs of children who come to dramatherapy, irrespective of their specific problems are:

- A secure and equal relationship in which the children feel accepted as they are – by playing with them instead of just observing their activities.
- Clear physical boundaries – a carpet or cloth on which the play takes place defining the parameters of reality and fantasy – the play is contained but not restricted. The dramatherapist needs to have clear personal boundaries in order to help clients recognise their own, for example, when they are playing and when they are not.
- A clear contract of confidentiality. Who has to be told what happens in therapy, for example, who should be told if episodes of abuse are reported. Children need to know what is to be told and to whom.
- A need for the dramatherapist to listen while the children express themselves creatively in therapeutic play – they may never have felt they have been heard in the past.
- To be valued as a person and validated by the dramatherapist and possibly also by parents and teachers.
- To work at their own pace.
- To be trusted and believed.

Aspects of these needs are illustrated in the following vignette:

### Peter transforms the giant

*Peter was five years old, came from a dysfunctional family and had been frequently deprived of playthings as a punishment.*

*He was bullied by his big brother and was frightened by older children at school. His play in therapy consisted of alternately being a monster and the slayer of monsters. One day he was drawing an ugly giant with a large yellow face. He decided that was too nice a colour for a giant and painted it blue instead. Peter was surprised when the giant's face turned green. He called it 'magic' and started to experiment by mixing other colours. He discovered that changing the colour of pictures alters their appearance, making them more or less threatening as required. In learning about colours, he also had some insight into transformation.*

When working dramatherapeutically with children, it is really important that, outside the agreed roles taken in any enaction, the dramatherapist remains true to the real relationship with the child as it is in the therapy room. It is easy to be cast in the role of parent or teacher and respond to it. If this happens, both child and therapist are likely to become confused and react in an unhelpful manner by, for example, responding 'as if' the therapist were some other person in the child's life.

## *Working with offenders – dramatherapy and the criminal justice system*

The term 'offender' is applied to anyone who has been found by the courts to have broken the law. The term covers a whole range of offences from, for example, driving whilst under the influence of drugs or alcohol, criminal damage, theft to murder. Some are placed under the care of the probation service to a period of supervision and/or rehabilitation and may be ordered to make amends for their behaviour by working in, and for, the community for a specific period. Others are detained in secure environments such as special units for young offenders, open prisons and secure prisons. Offenders who have mental health problems in the UK are usually sent to special forensic psychiatric units within the National Health Service. Nevertheless, most prisons have a hospital wing in which psychiatric assessments can be made. For more severe psychiatric problems resulting in gross antisocial behaviour, there are special hospitals such as Broadmoor, Rampton and Ashworth.

Prison services are for the punishment and/or rehabilitation of offenders who are mentally healthy. They are staffed by prison officers, there may be visiting therapists, but they are not intended to be therapeutic institutions – although some prisons do now make allowance for rehabilitation as people come to the end of their sentence.

Both prisons and forensic units are institutions where the environment has to be considered in relation to the issue with which dramatherapists and clients wrestle in their efforts to produce change. One danger is that it is very easy for the therapist to take up an 'anti-establishment' stance when up against the punitive side of prison or forensic work. It is very important to work alongside the establishment without commending it or joining the prisoners against it!

Therapists who work in forensic units or prisons need to be fully aware of the system and the pitfalls therein. This is why it is most important that they are supervised by someone who is also familiar with the services and knows the organisational problems well.

It is possible that people suffering from a personality dysfunction (see Chapter 8) may be sent to prison because these disorders are not considered as treatable mental disorders. In the UK there is currently discussion as to the appropriate measures and legislation for such people, but as yet, no change in the current legislation, the Mental Health Act 1983.

Much depends on the nature of the crime, availability of beds and the suitability of the client for a particular form of management. Williams-Saunders (2000) has written about work in this field in her book *Life within Hidden Worlds: Psychotherapy in Prisons*. Also, Thompson (1998) has edited a book on the use of drama and theatre in prisons which may be useful to the reader.

### Dramatherapy in prison

The punitive and custodial nature of prisons creates a particular and characteristic environment that has to be considered and taken into account in relation to dramatherapy. For example, the disempowerment resulting from being locked up may, at least for some prisoners who have had an abusive or dysfunctional childhood, needs to be considered. Williams Saunders (1997); refers to a past sense of being emotionally 'locked in' which the dramatherapist needs to take into account.

Forensic units and special hospitals are clearly part of the mental health service, so it is easy to make a case for psychotherapy (and therefore dramatherapy) as an appropriate intervention for people in the care of these institutions. The suitability of drama-therapy for those within the prison service is harder to establish. The purpose of prison is not therapy and there may be doubts and misunderstandings by both staff and offenders about its purpose. As Stamp (1998: 93) asks 'much as I feel that dramatherapy was use-ful, why should the prison authorities and even the prisoners them-selves agree?' She goes on to make the case, stating:

> ... 'being inside' ... can be seen as a time of change; participating in dra-matherapy in prison can be a medium for this. It can help towards reha-bilitation, looking at the change between life inside and life outside. It can be a way of looking at the issues that might be leading to a repetition of offending. It can be an opportunity to explore personal issues and anx-ieties that stem from early life. It can be particularly useful because it does not have to tackle these issues directly; they can be worked with indirectly, through techniques such as role play. (1998: 94)

Dramatherapists are being increasingly employed in the prison services and there is a development of expertise in this area of work.

### Dramatherapy in forensic units

Forensic units are hospitals and are staffed by nurses. Care regimes are graded, starting with a firm routine, clear boundaries and sched-uled activities. Clients with different mental health problems from each other may be simultaneously resident in the same forensic unit. This situation can be compared to a hospital, in that there would be people who are chronically ill, acutely ill and those who are ready for rehabilitation. A forensic unit will have the usual amenities for education, recreation, occupational therapy and, increasingly, arts therapies (that is one or more of dramatherapy, art therapy, music therapy and dance movement therapy). A dramatherapist may be employed to work in a forensic unit as part of a team or on an indi-vidual basis.

The needs of clients in a forensic unit will depend on their mental state. However, because of the element of compulsion, there may well be hostility against the environment (the criminal justice system, the institution and/or the staff) to be considered before dra-matherapy can begin. Most clients are sent to forensic units via the courts and judicial system. Some may be detained under the Mental Health Act 1983 and transferred from district psychiatric services where they have been found to be unmanageable or dangerous. A custodial sentence of imprisonment is a specified length of stay.

Compulsory treatment under the Mental Health Act for serious offences like homicide and arson are not time limited and are subject to clinical progress and sometimes Home Office control. Some clients consider this unfair and feel they would have had a shorter period of detention if they had been given a prison sentence. This may well be true and it is frequently an obstacle that has to be overcome before therapy can start in earnest. There is often also antagonism towards the institution that appears to be imposing restraint and to have a prison-like atmosphere. It may take several sessions to work through these feelings either on a group or individual basis.

It is possible that people suffering from a personality dysfunction, learning difficulties or even psychosis are sent to prison because, as described earlier, they are not recognised as suffering from mental disorders. Once they are there, they present a serious problem of management to the prison authorities.

The principle needs of offenders who come to dramatherapy are:

- A secure environment and confidentiality contract, the same as any other client
- Clear boundaries of space, privacy and an understanding that the role of the therapist is not that of a prison officer
- Exploration of feelings, particularly those about compulsory detention
- If there is no mental health problem and the offender is worried by their offence, an exploration of their crime and their attitude towards it
- Researching and practising new roles and life skills by role play and social skills training.

As indicated above, there may be resistance to therapy from some clients in forensic units. This will need time for exploration. Unlike hospitals where brief therapy is often the rule, the clients of forensic units are usually resident for longer periods which allows time to work through any resistance.

### Ronald's cage

*Ronald was a young man who had been involved in an attempted robbery. He had a disturbed childhood and been in a variety of institutions. At the time he was sentenced, the court took the view that Ronald was mentally unwell and that this had contributed to his criminal behaviour. Rather than sending him to prison, Ronald was sent to a forensic unit for treatment. When he joined the dramatherapy group at the forensic unit, Ronald was recovering from a depressive phase in which he had attempted to cut his wrist. He repeatedly expressed his anger at being in the forensic unit for an unspecified time whilst his peers who had been on trial with him had served their brief prison sentence and been released. Other group members joined with him in protesting about the unfair judicial system, the limitations of the forensic unit and in expressing anger at society in general.*

*The dramatherapist suggested each group member find an image for the word 'institution'. Most members described grey and oppressive buildings, but Ronald's image was of a cage, with people poking knives through the bars at the animals within. The images were not explored at the time, but further anger was expressed then and in later sessions. When the group had established a sufficient degree of trust to look at personal issues, Ronald returned to his image. His feelings when he was inside the cage were of oppression, anger and fear. When he was outside, poking knives through the bars he felt elated that he was exacting retribution for the way he had been treated.*

*Ronald went through a long, slow process of imagery and dramatic exploration before he could associate his troubled childhood with his present depressive state. The feelings of deprivation and loss he had experienced as a child had contributed to his feelings of inadequacy and anger towards society. When he was inside the cage he was dispirited and vulnerable. When he was outside the cage he wanted to get his own back on a system that he felt had let him down.*

At the commencement of a new dramatherapy group, it is sometimes necessary to allow continued expression of controlled or modified anger before attempting to look for any underlying feelings. The dramatherapist in the above example worked with closed groups for blocks of ten sessions, after which group membership was reviewed. The first five sessions usually consisted of the expression of anger and creating trust in the group before any personal work could be achieved. By midway through the sessions, people had established some trust in the dramatherapist and other group members and were able to work on personal issues. When the dramatherapist became aware of what was happening, she took it into account and built it into the pattern for future dramatherapy groups.

## Dramatherapy with substance abusers

The abuse of illicit drugs, inhalants and alcohol create both physical and behavioural problems as well as addictive dependency. Dramatherapy has a role in the treatment and rehabilitation of people who experience substance abuse related problems. For example, Mackay (1996: 164–6) describes her work with new entrants to a detoxification programme where she worked to increase their roles, aid the release of roles that were no longer of use to them and explore a range of expressive responses. This work culminated in a performance to others associated with the institution.

Apart from when expressing a desire to overcome the dependency, there are five main stages when substance abusing clients seek, or are sent for help. These are:

- During acute intoxication, which can range from an alcoholic or drug induced emotional 'high' to delirium, psychosis or coma
- When experiencing withdrawal symptoms of a physical nature – sweating, vomiting, diarrhoea – and also emotional symptoms of anxiety, depression and general distress
- In a transitory period of psychosis as a result of the intoxication
- At the onset of an incipient psychosis that has been precipitated by the drug usage
- When expressing a desire to address the addiction and subsequent dependency.

Dramatherapy may be effective in the treatment of the psychosis, but the most common involvement would be the latter stage of rehabilitation from addiction. It is at this point that clients may wish to address life situations that have led to their substance dependency. There is also a need to establish new roles and consequently behaviour that will strengthen their desire to free themselves from addictive tendencies. Mackay, in the work briefly described above, encouraged her participants to experiment with the spontaneous playing of roles not normally associated with drug addiction – 'For example, the teacher, the caring parent, the counsellor, the safely aggressive and autonomous being' (1996: 164).

## Some other ways in which dramatherapy can be helpful

Most of the two preceding chapters have been about dramatherapy with client groups. It is usual to think in terms of people sharing characteristics and needs. However, dramatherapy is just as useful when thinking in terms of 'problems'. For example, dramatherapy may be indicated when any person is vulnerable, requires support or needs to make some adjustment in life. What follows is a brief indication of other areas in which dramatherapy may play a part.

### Primary prevention
Family or personal history can indicate vulnerability and the potential for breakdown. If a client seeks help when problems are just arising, it is possible to avert the creation of a major incident. Or in the event of some crisis having already arisen the person may be helped to adjust to what has happened. Bereavement counselling may preclude a later depressive illness. Family therapy or counselling can prevent break-up or ease any consequential problems that may arise from dysfunctional relationships. Clients who spend time as in-patients can be helped to re-adjust to independent living by learning the social skills and roles they will need on their return to the community. The development of social skills, stress management and self-esteem also contribute to the prevention of future problems.

### Support
A client who has specific problems can benefit by support from other people who share the same difficulties, whom they may find in a dramatherapy group. People who share the same problems such as anxiety, depression, eating disorders, loneliness or divorce from reality often require some help after clinical treatment has terminated. Dramatherapy is an excellent tool for creating a supportive group of individuals, encouraging self-help and mutual caring.

This may shorten a period of disability and can also be seen as a form of prevention of chronicity. All this indicates the value of specialised groups which dramatherapists try to provide whenever it is possible.

### Adaptation to disability
Both physical illness and mental health problems can leave a residue of disability. It requires time, perseverance and support to adjust to a different way of living be it an artificial limb, hearing or sight impairment or mental disturbance. In the same way that a person has to adjust to tinnitus, it may be necessary for another individual to come to terms with hearing voices or disturbed concentration. Although this is not therapy in a clinical sense, it is an essential part of rehabilitation.

This chapter is a brief description of dramatherapy as it exists in the UK today. It is not the total scene by any means. In fact, the book itself is intended simply to introduce dramatherapy as a profession, it cannot be all-embracing as the profession is still young and, as yet, still developing into different sectors. However, it does give some insight into the most common areas of employment and the challenges that dramatherapists and clients alike have to face.

# 10

---

# CONCLUSION

This book is an introduction to the basic principles of drama-therapy. There are many more books written on the subject, some of which are listed in 'Suggestions for further reading'. The experiences of many people have contributed to its professional development and its present format. Dramatherapy has moved forward considerably since the first exploratory sessions. It is now a recognised profession with its own university training courses at Masters level (see Chapter 1). The Health Professions Council (HPC) consults the British Association of Dramatherapists on professional issues and some dramatherapists act as HPC 'partners' sitting on various committees and visiting training courses to ensure they adhere to the agreed standards.

New posts are gradually being created in the National Health Service, Social Services, Prison Services and Education, to name but a few. As dramatherapy continues to develop, new areas of practice arise. For example, the trend to treat people in the community rather than hospital, the treatment of offenders outside of prison and enlarged services for children and older people all make way for new ideas and ways of working.

The trend in the health and social services now is towards prevention as well as healing. Prevention may be a new area for dramatherapists but it has so far been the prerogative of educationalists. This raises the question of the boundaries of both therapeutic and preventative measures. Drama has been used to highlight health, social and political issues in the past (see Chapter 1). So are therapy and education growing closer together in practice? That is a question for continued debate but there is no doubt that dramatherapy is widening its perimeters. Sometimes a dramatherapist works in liaison with a theatre company that is aiming to inform on topics of health and social welfare and together they form an accurate picture.

There is an increased interest in research, and the change to a Master of Arts degree as an entrance to the profession will extend the number of papers written on the subject. Students commence their training with information about research methods, and are encouraged to validate their practice. This should encourage an enquiring profession for the future. Collaboration with the other arts therapies continues to take place with an increasing number of therapists working as a cohesive team, the unification makes for a stronger professional body and broader horizons. There is increasing interest in the European Consortium for Arts Therapies Education (ECArTE) with more universities both in Europe and the UK joining the partnership. This heralds more research, contact with universities overseas and the sharing of knowledge in their biannual conferences. Such encounters can only advance the development of the profession.

# SUGGESTED FURTHER READING

Bannister, A. (1997) *The Healing Drama*. London: Free Association Books.

Casson, J. (2004) *Drama, Psychotherapy and Psychosis: Dramatherapy and Psychodrama with People who Hear Voices*. Hove: Brunner-Routledge.

Cattanach, A. (1992) *Dramatherapy for People with Special Needs*. London: A&C Black.

Chesner, A. (1995) *Dramatherapy for People with Learning Disabilities*. London: Jesssica Kingsley.

Emunah, R. (1994) *Drama Therapy Process, Technique, and Performance*. New York: Brunner/Mazel.

Gersie, A. (1996) *Dramatic Approaches to Brief Therapy*. London: Jessica Kingsley.

Gersie, A. (1997) *Reflections on Therapeutic Storymaking*. London: Jessica Kingsley.

Grainger, R. (1990) *Drama and Healing: The Roots of Dramatherapy*. London: Jessica Kingsley.

Grainger, R. (1995) *The Glass of Heaven*. London: Jessica Kingsley.

Jenkyns, M. (1996) *The Play's the Thing*. London: Routledge.

Jennings, S. (1987) (1992) (1997) *Dramatherapy, Theory and Practice: Volumes 1, 2 & 3*. London: Routledge.

Jennings, S., Cattanach, A., Mitchell, S., Chesner, A. and Meldrum, B. (1994) *The Handbook of Dramatherapy*. London: Routledge.

Jones, P. (1996) *Drama as Therapy, Theatre as Living*. London: Routledge.

Landy, R. (1986) *Drama Therapy*. Springfield, IL: Thomas.

Landy, R. (1993) *Persona and Performance*. London: Jessica Kingsley.

Mitchell, S. (1996) *Dramatherapy Clinical Studies*. London: Jessica Kingsley.

Pearson, J. (ed.) (1996) *Discovering Self through Drama and Movement: The Sesame Approach*. London: Jessica Kingsley.

Wilkins, P. (1999) *Psychodrama*. London: Sage.

# REFERENCES

Alcock, M. (2003) 'Refugee trauma – the assault on meaning', *Psychodynamic Practice*, 9 (3): 291–306.

Andersen-Warren, M. (1996) 'Therapeutic theatre', in S. Mitchell (ed.), *Dramatherapy Clinical Studies*. London: Jessica Kingsley.

Anderson-Warren, M. (2000) 'Self disclosure and disguise: dramatherapy and masks', in R. Grainger and M. Anderson-Warren, *Practical Approaches to Dramatherapy, The Shield of Perseus*. London: Jessica Kingsley.

Artaud, A. (1970) *The Theatre and its Double* (trans. V. Cordi). London: John Calder.

Bannister, A. (1997) *The Healing Drama*. London: Free Association Books.

Bannister, A. (1998) 'Role reversal: when the protagonist is a survivor of abuse', *British Journal of Psychodrama and Sociodrama*, 13 (1 & 2): 45–55.

Bion, W. (1961) *Experiences in Groups and Other Papers*. London: Tavistock.

Black, D., Newman, M., Harris-Hendricks, J. and Mezey, G. (eds) (1997) *Psychological Trauma: A Developmental Approach*. London: Gaskell.

Blatner, A. and Blatner, A. (1988a) *The Art of Play*. New York: Human Sciences Press.

Blatner, A. with Blatner, A. (1988b) *Foundations of Psychodrama: History, Theory & Practice*. New York: Springer.

Boal, A. (1979) *The Theatre of the Oppressed*. London: Pluto Press.

Boal, A. (1994) in M. Schutzman & J. Cohen-Cruz (eds), *Playing Boal*. London: Routledge.

Braun, E. (1982) *The Director and the Stage*. London: Metheun.

Buckley, T. (1992) *The Poetics of Aristotle*. London: Prometheus.

Butcher, S.H. (1923) *Aristotle's Theory of Poetry and Fine Art with a critical text translation of THE POETICS* (4th edn). London: Macmillan.

Casson, J. (1984) 'The therapeutic dramatic community ceremonies of Sri Lanka', *Dramatherapy*, 7 (2): 11–18.

Casson, J. (2004) *Drama, Psychotherapy and Psychosis: Dramatherapy and Psychodrama with People who Hear Voices*. Hove: Brunner-Routledge.

Cattanach, A. (1994a) 'The developmental model of dramatherapy', in S. Jennings, A. Cattanach, S. Mitchell, A. Chesner and B. Meldrum (eds), *The Handbook of Dramatherapy*. London: Routledge.

Cattanach, A. (1994b) 'Dramatic play with children: the interface of dramatherapy and play therapy', in S. Jennings, A. Cattanach, S. Mitchell, A. Chesner and B. Meldrum (eds), *The Handbook of Dramatherapy*. London: Routledge.

Cattanach, A. (1994c) *Play Therapy: Where the Sky Meets the Underworld*. London: Jessica Kingsley.

Cattanach, A. (1996) *Drama for People with Special Needs* (2nd edn). London: A&C Black.

Chesner, A. (1994a) 'An integrated model of dramatherapy and its application with adults with learning disabilities', in S. Jennings, A. Cattanach, S. Mitchell, A. Chesner and B. Meldrum (eds), *The Handbook of Dramatherapy*. London: Routledge.

Chesner, A. (1994b) 'Dramatherapy and psychodrama: similarities and differences', in S. Jennings, A. Cattanach, S. Mitchell, A. Chesner and B. Meldrum (eds), *The Handbook of Dramatherapy*. London: Routledge.

Clare, R. (1998) 'Creating drama through advanced improvisation in prison', in J. Thompsom (ed.), *Prison Theatre: Perspectives and Practices*. London: Jessica Kingsley.

Courtney, R. (1986) *Play, Drama and Thought*. New York: Cassell & Collier Macmillan.

Cox, M. (1992) *Shakespeare Comes to Broadmoor*. London: Jessica Kingsley.

Dekker, K. (1996) 'Why oblique and why Jung?', in J. Pearson (ed.), *Discovering the Self Through Drama and Movement: The Sesame Approach*. London: Jessica Kingsley.

Department of Health (2004) *Advice on the decision of the European Court of Human Rights in the case of HL v. UK (The Bournewood case)*. London: HMSO.

Drury, N. (1989) *The Elements of Shamanism*. Dorset: Element Books.

Duggan, M. and Grainger, R. (1997) *Imagination, Identification and Catharsis in Theatre and Therapy*. London: Jessica Kingsley.

ECArTE (1999) *A Directory of European Training Courses*, available from ECArTE c/o Sarah Scoble, School of Applied Psychosocial Studies, University of Plymouth, Faculty of Health and Social Work, Millbrook Lane, Topsham Road, Exeter EX2 6ES.

Else, G. (1965) *The Origin and Early Form of Greek Tragedy*. Cambridge, MA: Harvard University Press.

Emunah, R. (1994) *Acting for Real*. New York: Brunner/Mazel.

Farmer, A., Eley, T.C. and Mcguffin, P. (2005) 'Current strategies for investigating the genetic and environmental risk factors for affective disorders', *British Journal of Psychiatry*, 186: 179–81.

Finkelhor, D. (1988) 'The trauma of child sexual abuse', in G. Wyatt and G. Johnson Powell (eds), *Lasting Effects of Child Sexual Abuse*. London: Sage.

Fulford, K. (1989) *Moral Theory and Medical Practice*. UK: Cambridge Press.

Gersie, A. (1991) *Storymaking in Bereavement: Dragons Fight in the Meadow*. London: Jessica Kingsley.

Gersie, A. (1997) *Reflections on Therapeutic Storymaking: The Use of Stories in Groups*. London: Jessica Kingsley.

Gersie, A. and King, N. (1990) *Storymaking in Education and Therapy*. London: Jessica Kingsley.

Gil, E. (1991) *The Healing Power of Play: Working with Abused Children*. New York: Guilford Press.

Goldberg, D. and Huxley, P. (1992) *Common Mental Disorders*. London: Routledge.

Grainger, R. (1990) *Drama and Healing: The Roots of Dramatherapy*. London: Jessica Kingsley.

Grainger, R. (1995) *The Glass of Heaven*. London: Jessica Kingsley.

Greenfield, S. (1997) *The Human Brain: A Guided Tour*. London: Weidenfeld & Nicholson.

Grotowski, J. (1968) *Towards a Poor Theatre*. London: Metheun.

Gunzburg, J. (1997) *Healing Through Meeting*. London: Jessica Kingsley.

Hare, A.P. and Hare, J.R. (1996) *J.L. Moreno* in Key Figures in Counselling and Psychotherapy Series, London: Sage.

Harrison, J. (1913) *Ancient Art and Ritual*. London: Williams & Norgate.

Hartnoll, P. (1985) *The Theatre: A Concise History*. London: Thames & Hudson.

Hasan, G. (1998) *Solomon's Ring: The Life and Teachings of a Sufi Master*. Walnut Creek, CA: Altamira Press.

Hodgkinson, P. (2000) 'Post-traumatic distress disorder', in C. Feltham and I. Horton (eds), *Handbook of Counselling and Psychotherapy*. London: Sage.

HPC (Health Professions Council) (2004) Partner Manual. London: HPC. www.hpc-uk.org

Hunningher, B. (1955) *The Origin of Theatre*. Amsterdam: Em Querido.

Jacobs, M. (1988) *Psychodynamic Counselling in Action*. London: Sage.

Jenkyns, M. (1996) *The Play's the Thing*. London: Routledge.

Jennings, S. (1990) *Dramatherapy with Families, Groups and Individuals: Waiting in the Wings*. London: Jessica Kingsley.

Jennings, S. (1993) *Playtherapy with Children: A Practitioner's Guide*. Oxford: Blackwell Scientific.

Jennings, S. (1994) 'What is dramatherapy? Interviews with pioneers and practitioners', in S. Jennings, A. Cattanach, S. Mitchell, A. Chesner and B. Meldrum (eds), *The Handbook of Dramatherapy*. London: Routledge.

Johnson, D.R. (1992) 'The dramatherapist "in-role"', in S. Jennings (ed.), *Dramatherapy Theory and Practice 2*. London: Routledge.

Jones, P. (1996) *Drama as Therapy: Theatre as Living*. London: Routledge.

Joseph, J. (2003) *The Gene Illusion: Genetic Research in Psychiatry and Psychology Under the Microscope*. Ross-on-Wye: PCCS Books.

Lahad, M. (1992) 'Storymaking: an assessment method of coping with stress: six-piece storymaking and BASIC Ph', in S. Jennings (ed.), *Dramatherapy Theory and Practice 2*. London: Routledge.

Landy, R. (1986) *Drama Therapy*. Springfield, IL: Charles C. Thomas.

Landy, R. (1992) 'One-on-one. The role of the dramatherapist working with individuals', in S. Jennings (ed.), *Dramatherapy Theory and Practice 2*. London: Routledge.

Landy, R. (1993) *Persona and Performance*. London: Jessica Kingsley.

Landy, R. (1996) *Essays in Dramatherapy*. London: Jessica Kingsley.

Langley, D. (1995/6) 'An interview with Peter Slade', *Dramatherapy* 17 (3): 2–6.

Langley, D.M. and Langley, G.E. (1983) *Dramatherapy and Psychiatry*. London: Croom Helm.

Langley, G.E. (2004) 'Serjeant Musgrave's disease', *Journal of Medical Humanities* 30 (2): 74–8.

Lemma, A. (1996) *Introduction to Psychopathology*. London: Sage.

*Making Decisions* (2003) A pamphlet issued by the Lord Chancellor's Department. London: HMSO.

MacKay, B. (1996) 'Brief dramatherapy and the collective creation', in A. Gersie (ed.), *Dramatic Approaches to Brief Therapy*. London: Jessica Kingsley.

Marineau, R. (1989) *Jacob Levi Moreno 1889 – 1974*. London: Routledge.

McCarthy, J. (2001) 'Post-traumatic stress disorder in people with learning disability', in *Advances in Psychiatric Treatment Vol. 7*. Royal College of Psychiatrists.

Mearns, D. and Thorne, B. (2000) *Person-Centred Therapy Today: New Frontiers in Theory and Practice*. London: Sage.

Meekums, B. (2002) *Dance Movement Therapy*. London: Sage.

Meldrum, B. (1994) 'Evaluation and assessment in dramatherapy', in S. Jennings, A. Cattanach, S. Mitchell, A. Chesner and B. Meldrum (eds), *The Handbook of Dramatherapy*. London: Routledge.

Milne, A.A. (1986) *The Complete Winnie-the-Pooh*. London: W. H. Smith & Son.

Mitchell, S. (1992) 'Therapeutic theatre: a para-theatrical model of dramatherapy', in S. Jennings (ed.), *Dramatherapy Theory and Practice 2*. London: Routledge.

Mitchell, S. (1994) 'The theatre of self expression: a "therapeutic theatre" model of dramatherapy', in S. Jennings, A. Cattanach, S. Mitchell, A. Chesner and B. Meldrum (eds), *The Handbook of Dramatherapy*. London: Routledge.

Moreno, J.L. (1977) *Psychodrama: Volume 1*. Beacon, NY: Beacon House.

Muss, D. (1991) *The Trauma Trap*. London: Doubleday.

Napaljarri, P. and Cataldi, L. (eds) (1994) *Yimikirli: Walpiri Dreamings and Histories*. San Francisco, CA: Harper Collins.

Newnes, C., Holmes, G. and Dunn, C. (1999) *This is Madness: A Critical Look at Psychiatry and the Future of Mental Health Services*. Ross-on-Wye: PCCS Books.

Newnes, C., Holmes, G. and Dunn, C. (2001) *This is Madness Too: Critical Perspectives on Mental Health Services*. Ross-on-Wye: PCCS Books.

Nichols, M. and Zax, M. (1977) *Catharsis in Psychotherapy*. New York: Gardner Press.

Pearson, J. (1996) *Discovering the Self through Drama and Movement: The Sesame Approach*. London: Jessica Kingsley.

Robertson, I. (1999) *Mind Sculpture*. London: Bantam Press.

Rogers, C.R. (1970) *Encounter Groups*. Harmondsworth: Penguin.

Romme, M. and Escher, S. (1993) *Accepting Voices*. London: MIND Publications.

Roose-Evans, J. (1970) *Experimental Theatre*. London: Routledge.

Sanderson, C. (1990) *Counselling Adult Survivors of Child Sexual Abuse*. London: Jessica Kingsley.

Sargant, W. (1957) *Battle for the Mind*. London: Heinemann.

Shuttleworth, R. (1987) 'A systems approach to dramatherapy', in S. Jennings (ed.), *Dramatherapy Theory and Practice for Teachers and Clinicians*. London: Croom Helm.

Singh, N.-G.K. (Trans.) (1995) *The Name of My Beloved: Verses of the Sikh Gurus*. San Francisco, CA: Harper Collins.

Slade, P. (1954) *Child Drama*. London: University of London Press.

Slade, P. (1995) *Child Play*. London: Jessica Kingsley.

Stamp, S. (1998) 'Holding on: dramatherapy with offenders', in J. Thompson (ed.), *Prison Theatre: Perspectives and Practices*. London: Jessica Kingsley.

Stanislavski, C. (1987) *Creating a Role*. London: Metheun.

Styan, J. (1996) *The English Stage*. Cambridge: Canto.

Thompson, J. (ed.) (1998) *Prison Theatre: Perspectives and Practices*. London: Jessica Kingsley.

Tuckman, B.W. (1965) 'Developmental sequence in small groups', *Psychological Bulletin*, 63: 384–99.

Watts, P. (1996) 'Working with myth and story', in J. Pearson (ed.), *Discovering the Self through Drama and Movement: The Sesame Approach*. London: Jessica Kingsley.

167

*Who Decides* (1997) A Consultation Paper Issued by the Lord Chancellor's Department. London: HMSO.

Wilkins, P. (1993) 'Psychodrama: a vehicle for self-integration?', *Journal of the British Psychodrama Association*, 8 (91): 5–17.

Wilkins, P. (1999) *Psychodrama*. London: Sage.

Wilkins, P. (2000) 'Storytelling as research', in B. Humphries (ed.), *Research in Social Care and Social Welfare: Issues and Debates for Practice*. London: Jessica Kingsley.

Williams Saunders, J. (1997) 'Living on the edge: reflections on the addictive and intoxicating nature of working in a women's prison'. Paper presented at the International Association of Forensic Psychotherapy (IAFP) conference London, May.

Williams Saunders, J. (2000) *Life Within Hidden Worlds: Psychotherapy in Prisons*. London: Karnac Books.

Wilshire, B. (1982) *Role Playing and Identity*. Bloomington, IN: Indiana University Press.

Winn, L. (1994) *Post Traumatic Distress Disorder and Dramatherapy*. London: Jessica Kingsley.

Winnicott, D.W. (1971) 'The concept of a healthy individual', in J.D. Sutherland (ed.), *Towards Community Health*. London: Tavistock.

Yardley-Matwiejczuk, K.M. (1997) *Role Play: Theory and Practice*. London: Sage.

Young, B. and Black, D. (1997) 'Bereavement counselling', in D. Black et al. (eds), *Psychological Trauma: A Developmental Approach*. London: Gaskell.

# INDEX